Simple Spells and Magickal Practices

Written by Amanda Godfrey

> This book is dedicated to my wonderful husband and son, who have immense patience for me and all the work I do. And to my parents and friends. Without all the love and support you all give me, in such beautiful and unique ways, I wouldn't be the person I am, doing what I love doing. Showering each of you with so much love and thanks.

Simple Spells and Magickal Practices
Copyright © Amanda Godfrey

First Edition 2024
Published by Aly's Books

www.alysbooks.com
Your Book | Our Mission

All rights reserved. No part of this book may be reproduced or transmitted in any form or by any means, electronic, mechanical, photocopying or otherwise without the prior permission of the publisher.

Images are sourced from Sam Parker's and club member's private collections.

In this book, the author has recreated events, locales and conversations from memories of them. The information in this book is based on the author's knowledge, experience and opinions. All photos in the book are from the author's private collection and other parties who have supplied to the author.

ISBN: 978-0-6459030-5-8

Contents

A Foot in Two Different Worlds	5
An Introduction to Spells and Magick	8

Healing Spells — 24
- Archangel Raphael Healing Spell — 24
- Assist Someone in Falling Pregnant Spell — 25
- Cinnamon Healing Spell — 26
- Clarity of Mind Spell — 28
- Diet Spell — 28
- Element Clearing and Healing Spell — 30
- Healing Grief Spell — 31
- Heart Healing Spell (Growing Self-Love) — 32

Personal Improvement Spells — 35
- Rebalancing My Life Spell — 35
- Connect to Universal Love Ritual — 36
- Courage and Bravery Spell — 37
- Expansion and Growth Spell — 39
- Inner Strength and Motivation Charm Bag — 40
- Motivation Spell — 41
- Problem-Solving Spell — 43
- Self-Love Spell — 44
- Creativity Faery Charm Spell — 45

Protection And Clearing Spells — 47
- Anubis Protection Oil Spell — 47
- Clearing Blockages Spell — 48
- Clearing Fears and Blockages Spell — 49
- Leaf Spell to Clear Negative Energy — 51
- Pheonix Rebirth Spell — 52
- Protection for My Home Spell — 53
- Road Opener Spell — 55

Psychic Spells — 57
- Add Energy to Spiritual Goals Charm Bag — 57
- Psychic Growth Spell — 58
- Psychic Activation Full Moon Magick — 60
- Seeking Answers/Guidance Spell — 61
- Amplify and Strengthen Intuition Charm Bag — 62

Relationship Spells — 64
- Clear Communication Spell — 64
- Communication Petition Spell — 65
- Conflict Resolution Spell — 66
- Forgiveness Spell — 68
- Happy Home Spell — 69
- Relationship Cord-Cutting Spell — 70

Wealth And Manifesting Spells — 72
- Add Energy to a Desire — 72
- Money Frog Spell — 73
- Money Basil Spell — 74
- Wish Box Manifesting Spell — 75
- Plant Manifesting Spell — 76

Invoking Blessings — 78
- Water Dragons — 79
- Fire Dragons — 80
- Earth Dragons — 81
- Air Dragons — 82
- Goddess Isis (Auset) — 83
- Goddess Brigid — 84
- God Poseidon — 85
- Angels — 86
- Archangel Michael — 87

A Final Word on Magick and Working Towards Our Goals — 89

Additional Correspondences — 91

A Foot in Two Different Worlds

What is it about trees, herbs, flowers and the idea of natural magick that continues to draw us in and enchant us? I honestly believe that a deeper, more advanced study and connection to natural magick, the seasons, the elements and the Sabbats is a beautiful way to discover another part of ourselves.

As Witches, we interact with the powers of creation and divinity every day, no matter where we live. The Deities and spiritual energies, the powers of the changing seasons, and the natural world that surrounds us enrich our lives. The longer we work with these energies and make time for our practice regularly, the deeper, more personal and meaningful our connection becomes.

I have studied and practised Witchcraft for more than 30 years now. And the longer I have been walking this path, the more I have come to understand about myself and the world around me. Even after all this time, I am still discovering new insights and having new experiences with Deities, elementals, energy, and more. I love that. I love that I can constantly learn and experience new things and that this is a never-ending journey of discovery and expansion.

I have also come to realise this path and its practices need to be incorporated regularly into our lives. The Witches of old we've all read about could devote their whole lives to their practice of witchcraft and didn't need to concern themselves with holding down a job or going to school as well. However, as modern Witches, we need to keep one foot in the mundane/physical world and one foot in the spiritual/natural world. We bridge these two worlds, doing an intricate dance to bring them together.

Our practices don't have to be complicated; in fact, I prefer simple practices as they mean I am focused less on superficial things and more on what I am doing, requesting or connecting to. Our spiritual and mundane worlds should not be two distinct areas we need to keep separate. I don't mean you have to be "out of the broom closet", telling everyone you meet you are a Witch. But it does mean that if you are having dramas at work, at school or in a relationship, you can use your connection and knowledge to aid yourself.

It also means you can't just call yourself a Witch because you are reading this book or some other book on witchcraft but then do nothing to practice anything you are reading about. Nor can you call yourself a Witch but then behave nothing like a Witch when you go outside your front door, going out of your way to be nasty, judgemental and uncaring to others.

Yep, there are those who would call me a "White Witch" or a "Wiccan" (rather than a Witch) because of the way I see this path. Some would say the path of a Witch includes curses, hexes and manipulation of others. I disagree; as a Witch, I have knowledge of these topics, but only so that I am able to help others. I do not believe a true Witch seeks to harm others. I believe that we are here to protect, heal, teach and take care of others.

I believe that, in everything, there exists good and bad, light and dark, black and white, positive and negative. Without having experienced sadness and grief, we could not experience the brilliance of joy and exhilaration. They are two sides of the same coin. Dark and light exist in everything; one cannot exist without the other. Magick—and energy itself—is a pure force in the Universe and, thus, I believe, is neutral. It is given a positive or negative focus by the person wielding that energy.

We need to understand that everything one single person does affects every other person in the Universe. This isn't just for spells and magick. We are energy, affecting the energy around us, which affects the energy around that, which affects the energy around that (you get the picture). We do a lot without even realising the effect we are truly having.

It is important to understand magick and energy as a whole to have any concept of what we might send out and what that, in turn, might do upon its return to us. Yes, that's right. Energy not only goes out affecting everything around you, but it also attracts more things to it and then also returns to us at some point. Energy is like a boomerang; it goes out there and does what it needs to and then returns with whatever that energy has attracted. In the case of when we want to manifest something specific, let's say, get a new job, we are hoping that energy will return with the opportunity for a new job that we want and love.

You may have heard of the Wiccan Rede, the Law of Three or the Law of Karma. These laws help us to keep this in mind. Particularly when you perform any type of magick work, you are going to cause some kind of change. How positive or negative is up to you. So, it is always good to look at what you intend to do and decide if any of your words, thoughts or deeds will harm or manipulate anyone. Remember that you are responsible for anything that you do.

The Law of Three, or the threefold law of return, means that whatever you do will not only come back to you but return to you threefold (times three). And I am here to tell you that the Universal Law of Three really does work. It is not some faerie tale made up to scare you into hopefully "doing the right thing". And no form of protection spell, amulet or disbelief in this law will stop it from working. That energy may not return today or tomorrow, but it will come back to you.

You might also be pleased to know that Witches don't worship the devil, and in fact, the devil is not included anywhere in our belief system. We believe all things in nature contain good and evil, but we do not believe in a devil, a Satan or a hell. Witches do not sacrifice animals, either. This concept goes against what we stand for. We believe that Deity is within all life, which therefore makes ALL LIFE sacred. As such, we acknowledge and have respect for every human being, every animal and plant that is in the world—everything that is living!

You don't have to consider yourself "special" or "psychic" to be a Witch either. Witches are men and women of all ages and backgrounds. We enjoy using our psychic gifts to help us connect with our higher self, other realms, deceased loved ones, and more. But your intuition is something you can develop if you want. You can also use such things as chanting, meditation, music, dance, invocation and ritual to help you tap into and work with these other realms and commune with those in spirit. And while we do honour spirit, the God and Goddess, we also recognise that the spirits of all entities in the Universe are equal (i.e. we, ourselves, are just as sacred as the Gods and Goddesses we call on!).

To be a Witch, you don't have to wear all black. You don't have to wear a certain type of dress or clothing. Nor do you have to wear a pentagram or specific jewellery. This path of a Witch is very personal, and I know it is this individual approach that can confuse those who get drawn to this path, especially at first. It is this personal approach that means I take no offence if you have a different opinion from mine about certain aspects I am discussing here. I am merely sharing my thoughts, beliefs and insights as a Witch who has walked this path for three decades. I've seen plenty of ideas and opinions, which I've both incorporated into my craft and plenty I've rejected. I have always encouraged my students to listen to what I have to say, take on board what resonates with them and leave what doesn't behind. I encourage you to do the same.

So, in a book on Witchcraft and magickal practice, we should define what I mean by magick.

I believe that magick is finding our connection to the Earth and all that is natural, alive and moving in the Universe! Magick is living in balance with the flow of life and knowing that we are a vital force within that flow. Magick is everywhere! It is all around us and also within us. It is in the trees, in the rain, in the stars, and in the sea. Magick is that spark that quickens a seed to rise from the soil and grow. It is also laughter, and joy, and wonder, and truth.

Magick is not greed, power or pretence . . . but it is real. It does exist, and it works. It is the essence of creation. I see the energies of magick as the energies of life itself. We "plug into" the divine energies all around us and use them to create or manifest something worthy and positive. Magick is a spiritual act to unite ourselves with our Deities and the natural world to better ourselves and the world around us.

Life becomes much more enchanted and sacred when consciously connected to this natural, wonderful energy. We are more aware of potential and possibility. We are more filled with hope for the future. And we are more able to create our dreams, heal ourselves (or others) and find peace within our hearts.

We don't have to live in the middle of nature or the bush to be a Witch and connect with magick. In fact, many of today's Witches are very likely to be living in city suburbs. But our physical location does not define us nor stop us from our practices. As Witches, we adapt and work with the magickal energies of nature that we find within our area, climate, and lifestyle. With this book, I hope to inspire you with more ways you can incorporate your magickal practices with where you are living and into your daily life. May my words help you to stand easily with a foot in both worlds so you don't feel like two separate people trying to live one life.

An Introduction to Spells and Magick

I believe magick happens when we are in flow with the universal energy that encompasses all things. This divine energy is all around us—in the trees, the rain, the stars, the sea, and even the chair you are seated on! It is in laughter, joy, and wonder and is the essence of all creation.

When we are connected to and in balance with this energy flow, we can create or manifest so many worthy and positive things in our lives.

Spells are a tool for directing universal energy. Spellcasting is the practice of moving natural energies to create change. It can be used to clear, cleanse, and release. We can use spells to improve and heal parts of ourselves, manifest desires, and enhance the world around us.

Spells are usually done through the use of spoken words accompanied by physical tools like candles, crystals, incense, herbs, etc. We combine our intent for a spell with items that hold appropriate energy that corresponds with that intent.

For example, let us say that we are working a healing spell. The spell might include spoken words to invite or affirm healing, a blue candle, a rose quartz crystal, lavender oil, sandalwood incense, and a worn charm in the shape of an ankh. The words and the items used all connect to the desired intent—in this case, they all relate to healing.

A spell can be considered a very "hands-on" approach to a situation. How many items you use or how elaborate the spell is doesn't really matter. It is you and your focused intent that makes the biggest difference. The problem is that many of us do not have the belief in ourselves to manifest simply through our will alone. So, we use the tools in our spell to help us focus and add energy to our requests.

To be the most successful with your spellwork, it is good to be aware of a number of things, which we will explore now. I encourage you to take the time to read through them before diving into the spell section of this book.

Your Sacred Space . . .

Since ancient times, people have been drawn to creating their own sacred spaces—from temples, pyramids, and churches to a simple altar made out of a tree stump in the middle of a forest.

Why? It is because it makes us feel closer to the divine.

When we create a special place like this and continue to use it for things like meditation, speaking to Divinities, affirmations and spells, it raises the vibrations of that space. As a result, it becomes much easier to make a connection because our vibrations lift to match the space we are working in.

Your own sacred space is easy to create at home and, for magickal workings, is often called an altar. Choose a special place in your home, preferably where others won't disturb you when you are using it, somewhere you can meditate close by. You can use a table, a shelf, a bedside table—whatever feels most suitable.

Decorate this sacred place with things that you love and are drawn to. You could use affirmation cards, favourite statues, photos, crystals, flowers, candles, plants, incense, etc.

If you are unable to have something permanent set up in your home, create a portable altar. Choose a box or container and fill it with the items you would put in your sacred space. Keep this box somewhere safe, and pull it out and set it up whenever you are meditating, doing spells, affirmations and manifestation work or simply feel the need to connect.

Meditation...

Meditation is essential for a Witch.

Successful spell casting requires good concentration and focus. Being able to visualise things we are trying to manifest clearly is also very helpful. These all can be enhanced with regular meditation.

Meditation is good for us on so many levels! It not only helps sharpen the mind but also helps to quiet the constant chatter so that we can be still enough to hear the voices of spirit, our elemental friends, Angels, Gods, Goddesses and any of the higher realms who would guide us.

This practice increases health by lowering blood pressure and decreasing stress levels. Meditation can alter moods, smoothing out highs and lows. It allows us to be more aware of our surroundings—to be more in the here and now—where we can make the most difference in our lives!

Anyone can meditate, and it does not involve severe concentration or twisting your body into certain positions. You do not have to be able to clear your mind and think of nothing. In fact, most meditations give you a point of focus. Meditation is about being relaxed and centred.

We can all make time for regular meditation, too. They don't need to be hour-long sessions. My usual routine consists of a short five or ten-minute meditation in the morning to start my day and finishes with a longer meditation before bed. My evening meditation can be anything from ten minutes up to an hour, depending on the day.

Working with Energy . . .

If you are doing spells, you need to be open to the idea (and preferably believe) that the universal energies we are working with ARE REAL. They might not be able to be physically seen, but they are within the Earth, all around us and within.

It is also good to understand that we create through our thoughts, words and actions. Of course, it is most potent to use all three together: what we think about, we are sending out to be made manifest; what we speak about, we are sending out to manifest; and what we do something about (take action toward), we are manifesting.

It is when what we think about, speak about, and act on are not in alignment that we cause ourselves the biggest drama! For instance, if you are doing spells for a new romantic relationship but mentally tell yourself you are useless when it comes to love and, on top of that, you are crying to girlfriends about how terrible being in a relationship can be, you are sending out mixed signals to Universe.

It is also interesting to look at the power of the written word. A simple candle spell method is to write what you want to bring into your life onto a scrap piece of paper and then burn it from the flame of a candle. How does this power work?

When we think about anything, each one of our thoughts is sent out into the Universe. Each one of those thoughts goes out and finds something that resonates with its energy, and it will grab hold of that and bring it back to you. The amount of emotion behind each thought will help decide how fast that thought goes about doing its work. The more emotional energy attached to a thought, the more power it has and the quicker it works. This is why it is essential to do spells that mean something to you; they will be far more effective, and you will see much faster results.

If we are in a confused state of being about something, then we will constantly be sending out a big "YES" to the Universe followed by a big "NO". An excellent example of this is if you are not convinced that you deserve that thing you've asked for (like a car or holiday) and have to reaffirm to yourself constantly that it is okay to have it. Each time you doubt, off goes your big "NO" again on its flight into the world!

On a happy note, positive thoughts are far more powerful than negative thoughts, so don't beat yourself up over it. Keep affirming what you want, and remember practice makes perfect!

When we write down our thoughts, we unscramble the confusion. Writing is an action that uses words with thoughts (and hopefully meaning/emotion) behind them. Writing is powerful stuff, no matter how you use it. Whether you write a letter expressing your heart-felt love for someone, write journal entries each night to help put your thoughts from the day into order, write a funny story to share with friends or write that abundance spell for the family. The written word is powerful.

Your Intention . . .

We need to add our intention to all aspects of our spells. To do this, we want to hold our candles, crystals and the other items we are using between both hands while we do three things:

- Visualise the outcome we want
- Feel the outcome we want AND
- Affirm the outcome we want (I like to use a statement or affirmation for this)

When we create an intention, it's important that we make it focused on the positive. We might have decided we need to do a spell and come up with our intent based on a worry or need we have when something isn't quite going right in our lives. Then we may fall into the trap of thinking in the negative.

For example, if we want to create something for protection, whether it is to protect our new car, protection for ourselves, or our home, the first thing we often think about is what we want to protect ourselves from. In the case of our car, it might be to prevent accidents and scratches.

The WRONG WAY to add this protection intent is to think about all the things you don't want to happen. For instance, you affirm things like, "This car will never be in an accident."

The RIGHT WAY to add this protection intent is to think about how you will be protected. You may see yourself having lots of happy driving experiences, your car staying shiny and new-looking, and focusing on feeling very safe and happy as you drive around all kinds of environments. Affirm things like, "I am always safe and happy as I drive in my car."

As long as it is positively focused, you can be as specific or as general with your intent as you like. For example, "I am always safe and happy as I drive in my car," might be considered quite specific. A more general affirming statement could be, "This car is protected."

You might like to write down your intent. In this way you can make sure to get it just right in your mind before using it. Plus, the statement you write down will be the perfect words to use to affirm while you add your intent.

Remember that you need to be clear in your request in order to get clear results in magick.

Dressing Your Altar

It is also important to dress your altar appropriately for any spell or magickal workings you are doing. This is a fancy way of saying, "Decorate your altar focused around your spell's intent."

Consider:

- Suitable colours for your altar cloths and candles that tie into your magickal intent, e.g. green for money, purple for intuition, pink for self-love.
- Fitting decorations, items, symbols and pictures that tie into your intent, e.g. you might add a bee, money tree, foreign coins and affirmation cards focused on abundance for a money spell.
- Items, symbols, statues and pictures associated with any Deity you are calling on. Note: It is good to research about the divinity you are calling on to know what these might be. You don't need all of them. Choose what you have or what makes sense to you.

You can be as elaborate or as simple as you like when it comes to dressing your altar. You might want to keep it very simple for some spells, selecting an appropriate coloured cloth along with your spell items. While, for other spells, you might have many items pertaining to your intent circling your spell items. The choice is yours.

Devising a Spiritual Plan . . .

Don't just throw spells at the problems that pop up in your life. Truly magickally-minded people usually consider an entire plan, of which spellwork is simply a part. A complete spiritual plan includes:

- Logical thought about the goal or situation—considering all the physical actions you can do around this, on both a magickal and mundane level. What action steps can you take in regard to this? What crystals or herbs could you be carrying or tucking somewhere to aid the situation? Do you need to cleanse a space to help? Is there someone you could talk to for mundane advice to help?

- Building positive reinforcement around you. What friends can you confide in who will help lift you up and advise you throughout the time ahead? Can you create a vision board of your desired outcome? Browse car catalogues if you are working on manifesting a car. Plan that perfect holiday you want. This all adds energy to aid in bringing it to you.

- Address belief blocks and reprogram your mind to accept success. If you doubt you are worthy of receiving what you have asked for, it's good to add daily affirmations, read books, or listen to podcasts to uplift you and remind you of your worthiness. This applies to any other belief block you might have to your request. Perhaps you believe you must work hard to earn money. Work on shifting that belief into a positive one which allows your request to flow in.

- Involve Divinity as much as possible. I adore working with Gods, Goddesses, Angels and elemental friends in my everyday life and all my manifesting. Speak to them daily. Ask for their help in everyday tasks. Thank them regularly. The more we connect with them, the stronger this connection becomes, which means we can see and feel their energy more easily.

- Take the blinkers off. Once you make a request to Universe, you need to be open to the opportunities that will come into your life. These can be unexpected opportunities that you had never entertained the idea of before. You don't have to say yes to all of them, but it certainly is counter-productive to keep saying "no" when Universe is opening doors for you. For instance, if you have done money magick and then continuously say "no" to all the overtime being offered to you and don't accept a friend trying to pay you back the money they owe, the avenues that money is trying to flow into you may suddenly halt.

Belief Blocks

Often, when we request something, part of the reason it hasn't manifested in our life \ of its own accord before now is there is a belief block in the way.

I have witnessed the worthiness belief block getting in the way many times. Let's say we ask for a job promotion, and, deep inside, we don't feel we deserve it, then doing a spell doesn't suddenly stop us from feeling unworthy. Instead, what I find happens is that Universe says,

"That is wonderful that you feel you are worthy enough to have this at last!" From there, you will likely find this belief block (in this example, worthiness) starts to be poked in your life. You may suddenly find a number of people or situations begin pushing your buttons, making you demonstrate how you ARE worthy.

If you start to get your buttons pushed and see a theme like this arise after doing a spell—believe it or not, this is a positive sign! It means Universe is working on your request. And you need to step up and show how this is no longer a blockage for you. Perhaps you start using an affirmation to help shift your mindset, carry a crystal that will help support the affirmative, stand up for yourself in some way, or do a healing ritual specifically focused on the issue. It all helps to dissolve the belief block and support your magickal request.

As a side note, it is also a good idea to use a statement like "this (your specific request) or better" in your spells to help ensure you are not putting a glass ceiling on your spell (which we tend to do when belief blocks are at play). This way, if Universe has better plans, then it has the scope to bring that in for you. Think what a difference it could make for things like selling your house with the average price you've asked for versus a brilliant price you never could have imagined, which universe has brought you instead!

How Long for My Spell to Manifest?

There is no hard and fast rule as to how long a spell will take to manifest.

I have encountered this rule of thumb many times in my research: small goals can take less time to manifest, and you can often see results within one moon cycle (approximately thirty days). Larger goals take longer (months or even a year).

Personally, I believe that the amount of time it takes for a spell to manifest depends more so on the person casting the spell—how strong their intent is, how focused they were throughout the spell, how much doubt and fear they have around their request, how much they believe they deserve what they have asked for, etc.

Your mindset can play a role in this, too; if you think it will take a long time to manifest, it often will. If you think it will be super-fast because you have requested it, then it can be! I once manifested my own home in around six months. My partner and I were both working casual jobs with next to no savings at the time. I suddenly decided the time was now. I had a lot of emotion behind this desire—the fence of our rental had fallen down, and our landlord wasn't in a hurry to fix it. My poor dogs were in temporary fencing, and our yard was now open to a public park! I jumped on every opportunity offered by Universe, and before we knew it, we moved into our own home.

I also believe that Universe has a say about what we are manifesting. Are all the pieces lined up, ready to fall into place to create what you are asking for? Have you been healing the belief blocks that were keeping this request at bay? Is it for your highest good that this request is realised? These things will all have an influence over how fast or slow the manifesting occurs.

Why Don't Spells Always Work?

Don't think that all is going to turn out exactly the way you had hoped or expected just because you are happily casting spells. Remember that there are many reasons why you might end up with a result you weren't expecting. This is not necessarily a "failure".

We don't always know why what we have requested hasn't been made manifest.

- Perhaps you haven't waited long enough.
- Perhaps you still have belief blocks that you haven't quite healed enough to allow your request in.
- Perhaps you have been sending out too many confused messages since doing your spell (remember, it's not only the spell itself that influences its energy).

Sometimes Universe has tried to give you your request, but you've had blinkers on and haven't seen it. Many times, I have taught classes where we have done a money spell, and I have had some students return later saying the money they wanted didn't come. However, when I ask them questions, we get to the bottom of it. For example, "Did you get offered any overtime or extra shifts at work?" To that, the answer is almost always "Yes". So, more money did try to come in, but they said "no" to the opportunities. And if you say "no" too many times when Universe is trying to bring you what you have requested, it stops trying. This doesn't mean you have to say "yes" to all the ways Universe tries to bring you what you have asked for. But it does mean you should accept more opportunities that present than you reject!

Universe knows better than we do when it comes to what will be right for us in any situation. Sometimes, it takes a different route to protect us. Other times, Universe knows we have bigger missions, larger goals, and more important activities that we should be doing, and so granting us this request may move us away from where we need to be.

Before You Cast a Spell . . .

Always remember the Wiccan Rede when deciding whether you will do a spell: "Bide the Wiccan Law ye must, In perfect Love and perfect Trust. Eight words the Wiccan Rede fulfil: An' ye harm none, do what ye will. What ye send forth comes back to thee, So ever mind the law of three, Follow this with mind and heart, Merry ye meet and merry ye part." -quote from the Wiccan Rede, author unknown.

The term "harm none" includes all living beings in the world, the planet itself, and, of course, you. So, to follow this code of ethics, you need to look at what you intend to do and decide if any of your words, thoughts or deeds will harm or manipulate anyone in any way. Remember that you are responsible for everything you do, and there is no spell, amulet or disbelief in the law that will protect you from this powerful Universal law. Everything you send out always comes back to you in some way. You are the one who will ultimately determine if it is positive or negative.

Casting spells on others: Whenever you decide to work any type of magick, it is essential to remember that you should not cast spells directly onto people that will make them do things against their free will. A common way I see people fall into this trap is when they want to attract a romantic partner. They decide that a particular person is meant for them and do spellwork with the specific intent to attract them. That is manipulation.

Rather than naming a specific person, it is better to list the attributes you are looking for in a partner. If there is someone in your life whom you admire, write down all the qualities that make them attractive to you and ask to manifest someone with those qualities. Doing spells that work against someone's free will breaks the Wiccan Rede and, therefore, creates consequences for you down the track. I have seen love spells done that end up with terrible results because of this.

Causing punishment: It is not your job to hand out punishments or "hurry up karma", no matter how bad you think the person is or how certain you are of what they have done. The Universe will deal with them when the time is right, and casting spells on them will only see to it that you end up entangled in their energy and karma. If in doubt, always look at what you can do to help heal yourself in the situation rather than focusing on the other person involved. It is far better to cast a spell releasing anger for yourself than throwing angry energy at someone.

Multiple spells: When working spells, it is best to focus on one spell at a time. There is no point in having five candles burning down, all for different reasons and trying to do various things on the same night. You won't have put as much energy and heart into each one as you would have if you had focused on a single spell. It's the energy, emotion and concentration that make magick work. The more you can pour into each spell, the more powerful that spell will be. So, if you have a list of things you would like to work on, prioritise that list and work on one thing at a time. You will be glad you did!

Seek Permission: If you are doing spells for other people (say a healing spell), it is a good idea to ask their permission. Obviously, if they have asked you to do the spell for them, then you have their permission. If you don't feel you can ask them directly, you could always tune in with meditation and ask their higher self for permission to work the magick. Sometimes, for reasons not obvious to us, the person will not accept healing or positive energy from us—and it is their right (free will) to refuse the help!

Seek Assistance: While you can certainly do spells on another person's behalf, for best results, I recommend getting them involved in the spell in some way. The person wanting the spell done will always have a stronger emotional connection to the outcome than you will have (you can want it for them, but they will REALLY want it for themselves!). And a stronger emotional connection always makes for stronger outcomes in your spellwork. These days, I tend to teach others how to do the spell for themselves rather than doing a spell for them.

Keep Your Magick Quiet: I do encourage you not to go around telling everyone about what spell you have just done! The negative thoughts and words of those who do not truly believe in you, your unlimited potential and the infinite magick of the Universe can limit your results. Not to mention, speaking about it too much is thought to lessen its power. To know, to dare, to will, and to be silent all have deep meanings in witchcraft teachings.

The Right Timing for Your Spells…

If your need is urgent, then you can work at any time of the day, night or month. However, if you have a little time up your sleeve to plan your spell, it certainly does add energy to align the timing appropriately.

Please know that NOT doing your spell at the "best energy" time of the month does not mean your spell won't work. To emphasise, if your spell is urgent, just do your spell at the time you need to. It won't take away from your spell.

Sometimes the nature of the spell you are intending to do can help dictate the timing. For example, a new beginnings spell can be done on:

- The first day of the month
- The first day of the year
- The first day of the week
- At dawn
- At the New Moon
- Any combination of the above (e.g. at dawn on the first day of the month)

Working with the energy of the SUN …

It's not just the Moon that has significant energy to add to our spells. The Sun also offers a great source of energy that we can work with for our magick. Some even consider the Sun a more instant form of energy to work with, whereas others consider the Moon slower and gentler.

Dawn

Timing: When the Sun is first getting up, the very start of the day.

Energy: This is the best time of day for new beginnings and bringing people and opportunities into your life.

Noon

Timing: Midday (12:00 hrs), the middle of the day.

Energy: This is a great burst of instant power, energy and success for your magick work. Noon is thought to be like the Full Moon, giving all intent a big boost of energy.

Dusk

Timing: When the Sun goes down at the very end of the day. It is usually marked by sunset, where we can see beautiful colours in the sky.

Energy: This is a great time for clearing and letting go. It is also considered a good time for reconciliation magick.

Working With the Energy of the MOON . . .

Dark Moon

Timing: The day before the New Moon, when there is no Moon visible in the sky.

Energy: Many, me included, consider this to be a time to rest and do no magick. Instead, we can use this time to be reflective and thoughtful and plan ahead. Others use this time to remove unwanted energies.

New Moon

Timing: When the Moon is a tiny sliver in the night sky. Just after the Dark Moon.

Energy: This is the perfect time for new beginnings and new projects. The New Moon amplifies our ideas, inspiration, and energy. This is the time to send out our hopes, dreams and wishes to the Universe—like planting a seed so they can grow. It is a time for growing, increasing, bringing energy in, activating, and renewing.

Waxing Moon

Timing: When the Moon is growing bigger—the period between the New Moon all the way through to the Full Moon.

Energy: This is a potent time for all kinds of growing magick. Waxing Moon energy puts energy behind increasing our money, happiness, health, fertility, or whatever we ask for. It is a great time to add energy to anything in your life—a time for building, creating, manifesting, enhancing, or healing.

Full Moon

Timing: When the Moon is a full round circle in the sky. The energy of the Full Moon is considered to last for about 3 days—the Full Moon day plus one day before and one day after.

Energy: This is the most well-known time for spellwork, as it is the most potent time for ALL MAGICK. The Full Moon will amplify and put a big boost of energy behind all intent, whether you are manifesting, healing or clearing out. Plus, this is a great day or night for initiating any kind of change in your life.

Waning Moon

Timing: When the Moon is growing smaller —the period between the Full Moon all the way through to the Dark Moon.

Energy: This energy is focused on letting go. It helps us to clear away what we no longer need or wish for in our lives and can help to release and remove pain, sorrow, or any destructive influences. This is an excellent time to do things like start a new diet or do some magick to aid us with losing weight!

Extending On This...

As mentioned above, we can work purely with the energy of Full Moon, Waning Moon etc. This works well. However, we can take this one step further by also working with the energy of the astrological sign the Moon is in.

The Moon shifts through all the astrological signs every lunar cycle (every month), sitting in each sign for approximately two and a half days before moving into the next. Each month, the New Moon is in a different sign, and the Full Moon is, too. All the astrological signs rule over and amplify different energies. So, if we work our magick at the time of the most appropriate moon phase and the astrological sign, we add greater layers of power to our magick.

The following is a general guide to help you with working with this:

Capricorn

When the Moon is in the sign of Capricorn, it is the best time to work magick for:
- structure/being organised
- career/reputation
- justice and legal matters
- relationships with fathers
- major life goals
- material concerns
- self-restraint

Also more powerful at this time are healing spells and rituals for:
- bones/skeletal system,
- teeth
- knees
- skin
- cutaneous system
- joints

Gemini

When the Moon is in the sign of Gemini, it is the best time to work magick for:
- communication
- writing and studies
- learning and understanding
- public relations
- searching for answers
- adaptability and multitasking
- dealing with siblings

Also more powerful at this time are healing spells and rituals for:
- shoulders
- arms
- hands
- speech
- bronchial tubes
- thymus
- lungs

Cancer

When the Moon is in the sign of Cancer, it is the best time to work magick for:
- peace and love
- emotions
- home-life and family
- protection
- intuition
- creativity
- feminine issues
- self-love

Also more powerful at this time are healing spells and rituals for:
- chest
- stomach
- diaphragm
- womb
- ribs
- digestive organs

Aquarius

When the Moon is in the sign of Aquarius, it is the best time to work magick for:
- creative expression
- independence and originality
- freedom
- problem-solving
- new perspectives
- intuition
- hopes and dreams
- groups and organisations
- breaking bad habits

Also more powerful at this time are healing spells and rituals for:
- calves and ankles
- tibia and fibula
- breath
- blood
- circulation

Leo

When the Moon is in the sign of Leo, it is the best time to work magick for:
- leadership
- courage and strength
- positivity
- self-esteem
- success and wealth in the home
- helping your talents to shine
- fertility
- your pets

Also more powerful at this time are healing spells and rituals for:
- upper back
- spine
- blood circulation
- spleen
- heart
- vital forces

Pisces

When the Moon is in the sign of Pisces, it is the best time to work magick for:
- intuition, divination and dreams
- personal development
- compassion and peace
- seeing the big picture
- music and creative arts
- inspiration
- imagination and visualisation

Also more powerful at this time are healing spells and rituals for:
- feet
- toes
- lymphatic system
- glandular system

Virgo

When the Moon is in the sign of Virgo, it is the best time to work magick for:
- finding solutions
- intellectual matters and thinking
- employment
- financial improvements
- self-improvement
- finding people, information and things
- study, exams, better grades
- health and dietary concerns

Also more powerful at this time are healing spells and rituals for:
- intestines
- nervous system
- abdominal organs
- spleen
- bowels

Aries

When the Moon is in the sign of Aries, it is the best time to work magick for:
- rebirth and new beginnings
- leadership
- self-reliance
- assertiveness and being fearless
- success
- spontaneousness
- energy levels
- will power

Also more powerful at this time are healing spells and rituals for:
- face
- head
- brain
- eyes
- teeth
- pineal gland

Libra

When the Moon is in the sign of Libra, it is the best time to work magick for:
- justice and the legal system
- partnerships and unions
- cooperation
- conflict mediation
- beauty and love
- friendship and being social
- communication
- karmic, spiritual, and emotional balance

Also more powerful at this time are healing spells and rituals for:
- lower back
- adrenals
- venous system
- lumbar
- nerves
- skin
- kidneys

Scorpio

When the Moon is in the sign of Scorpio, it is the best time to work magick for:
- psychic growth
- transformation
- ending connections
- getting to the bottom of a messy situation
- nurturing self
- working through emotions
- wisdom and reflection
- illumination

Also more powerful at this time are healing spells and rituals for:
- reproductive organs
- bladder
- colon
- urinary system
- prostate
- coccyx

Taurus

When the Moon is in the sign of Taurus, it is the best time to work magick for:
- money and material acquisitions
- trust, stability, and harmony
- long-term goals and projects
- determination
- success
- productivity and responsiveness
- artistic endeavours

Also more powerful at this time are healing spells and rituals for:
- throat
- neck
- jaw
- chin
- tonsils
- thyroid
- vocal cords
- ears

Sagittarius

When the Moon is in the sign of Sagittarius, it is the best time to work magick for:
- expansion
- legal matters
- publications
- optimism and keeping the faith
- self-mastery
- in-laws
- travel, especially long-distance
- sports
- metaphysics and seeking wisdom

Also more powerful at this time are healing spells and rituals for:
- liver
- thighs
- hips
- sciatic nerve
- arterial system
- pelvis
- sacrum

Healing Spells

Archangel Raphael Healing Spell

Bring healing for yourself to aid physical ailments and emotional or mental issues. This spell will also bring you some peace and calm or help you if you are struggling on any level.

Best Timing:

A Full Moon is ideal, especially if the Moon is in Virgo or when the Moon is in the sign most aligned to heal your ailment. However, this spell can be done at any time it is needed.

Required Items:

- A red candle and holder (green or white is a good substitute)
- A bloodstone or garnet crystal (tumbled works well)
- Frankincense incense, resin or essential oil (go with what you prefer to burn)
- A statue or image of Archangel Raphael

What to Do:

Archangel Raphael is a beautiful and powerful energy to call on for healing. He is the angel most considered in charge of all healing and is the special patron of physicians, nurses, pharmacists, and the ailing. His emblem is the fish. Raphael is often seen surrounded by the colour emerald green and is sometimes depicted holding a flask of medicine. We can call on Archangel Raphael whenever we need any kind of healing.

A good way to do this is, first of all, to have an image of him. You may find something on the internet, have an oracle card that represents him, or already have a statue. Choose something that resonates with you. Place your chosen image on your altar or sacred space.

Burn your preferred frankincense, and as you inhale the scent, charge your candle and crystal between two hands while seeing, feeling and affirming that you are full of health. See yourself full of vitality, healthy and happy. See/feel any ailments that have been causing an issue dissolve and disappear completely. You don't need to see how they are "cured", just that they are gone, and you are happy and healthy.

Then set up your candle ready to burn and place your crystal sitting at its base. When you are ready, light your candle and invoke Archangel Raphael. You can use your own words or say the following:

"Archangel Raphael,
You who are blessed with healer's grace,
I ask for your love and help now, please.
Fill my body with your emerald green light,

And with it, dissolve away all illness, discomfort and pain.
Bless me so that vibrant health increases within me each day.
With thanks and harm to none, so mote it be."

Allow your candle to burn all the way out alongside your image of Raphael and your crystal, both charging up in the energy beside the candle.

When the candle is finished, gaze at the candle wax for any messages. Allow your higher self to guide you as to any symbols you see might mean. Make sure to move your candle wax around and view it at different angles to get the most symbols, images and insight.

Any leftover wax can then be disposed of in the bin. You can carry your crystal on you or keep it beside your bed. This will help channel Archangel Raphael's healing energy to you over the coming days or weeks.

Assist Someone in Falling Pregnant Spell

For the best results, the couple trying to conceive should perform this spell together. Or at least try to have one of them participate in casting this spell. This spell is written from the perspective of you being the one wanting to be pregnant. You should adjust the spell slightly if you do it on someone's behalf.

Best Timing:

At a Full Moon, especially in the sign of Cancer or Pisces. You could also do this spell during a Waxing Moon or at a New Moon.

Required Items:

- A pink candle and holder
- The herb hawthorn
- The herb mugwort
- Rose petals
- Olive oil or rose essential oil
- Garnet, mookaite, and rose quartz crystals (tumbled or rough pieces work well for this)

What to Do:

Begin by gathering all your items together. Then set up your candleholder on your altar or sacred space with the crystals around the base. It is always good to decorate the altar with a nice, coloured cloth and one or two items that represent a baby for you, such as a magazine photograph of a baby or pregnant woman, baby booties, etc.

Mix the hawthorn and mugwort to make a blend. As you do this, focus on your intent. See/feel yourself pregnant or holding your newborn baby. Then pour the herbs onto a tray or board, spreading them out at least as long as your candle. Now, using your chosen oil, rub your candle in small circles, starting from the top and all the way to the bottom. As you do this, focus again on your intent. While the candle is slightly moist from the oil, roll it in the herb mix, ensuring the candle is at least lightly covered with some herbs.

Place your candle in the candleholder and sprinkle the rose petals in a circle around it. Focus on the loving connection your family has—the bond between husband and wife, the bond between mother, father, and baby.

The Egyptian Goddess Isis (Auset) is a mother archetype with a very loving and nurturing energy. You can call on her at this point to aid your spell:

"Beautiful Isis [Auset], we call on you now. We ask your assistance with conceiving, carrying, and bringing into the world a beautiful, healthy baby…"

Tell her the reasons you both want a child. See yourself as clearly as possible conceiving, carrying, and bringing a beautiful, healthy baby into the world. See/Feel/Affirm what it would be like. Take at least several minutes (or much longer) to do this.

When you feel ready, light the candle. With your heart and soul, know that this wish is already being taken care of. Leave your candle to burn all the way out. When the candle is finished, you could gaze at the candle wax for any messages. Allow your higher self to guide you as to any symbols you see might mean. Make sure to move your candle wax around and view it at different angles to get the most symbols, images and insight.

The following day, take any remaining melted wax and any leftover herbs and bury them under your bedroom window. If doing this for someone else, give the couple the parcel to bury under their bedroom window. Know that, from the Earth, all things grow.

Once you have finished, try not to focus on what you have just done or what you are trying to manifest. Put it out of your mind as best you can. Allow the Universe to work with this energy. When we think about it constantly, we hold onto the wish very tightly and do not release it to the Universe to do what it needs to create your wish.

To add to this:

I found creating an altar for my pregnancy on my bedside table really helpful.

I maintained this all the way through my pregnancy until my son was here with us! Put just a couple of items that represent pregnancy or a baby on this altar, including the crystals charged up from your spell. My main item was a fertility goddess statue with her big pregnant belly, and she was surrounded by the crystals. You can carry some of these crystals throughout the day and leave them on the altar at night if you like.

Cinnamon Healing Spell

This spell is perfect for adding healing to any physical ailments and mental or emotional issues. Send the healing energy to someone you know, or fill yourself with this powerful healing energy.

Best Timing:

A Full Moon or New Moon is ideal timing, but this spell can be done any time you need healing

Required Items:

- A piece of paper
- A cinnamon stick
- A picture of the person who will be receiving the healing (yourself or someone else)
- A small white cloth (about dinnerplate size is good)
- Some healing herbs. I suggest rosemary, eucalyptus and peppermint
- A healing crystal, I suggest bloodstone, garnet, shungite, or clear quartz
- A white tealight candle
- Eucalyptus essential oil

What to Do:

Centre yourself before writing your name, or the name of the person you want the healing to go to, on the piece of paper. You can add any symbols, words or statements around the healing if you wish to, or simply write the name. Fold the paper in half and wrap it around one end of your cinnamon stick.

Light the cinnamon stick. Get it smoking nicely, and take a few deep breaths, connecting with the scent (cinnamon is an all-around healing herb that helps put us into the right frame of mind for doing healing work).

When you feel ready, place the white cloth on your altar or sacred space. Keep yourself focused on your intent of sending healing or receiving healing as you do the following:

Pick up the picture of your healing recipient and place it in the centre of the white cloth. Then add your healing herbs on top of the image, focusing on the idea that you are immersing them in energy that will assist them with healing.

Next, add your healing crystal on top of the pile of herbs, once again reaffirming that you are adding healing energy to surround and assist them.

Now, you will wrap the picture, your herbs and crystal in the white cloth. Focus on this act, like you are gently wrapping the person you are sending healing to in a soft, comforting blanket of healing.

Place your tealight candle beside your now wrapped-up picture on your altar. Add a few drops of the eucalyptus oil to the top of your candle.

As you light your candle, say:

"Dearest God and Goddess who breathes life and vitality into us all,
Bless and charge this candle as a powerful magickal tool for healing."

Visualise the person you are sending healing to now. Visualise any illness being drained out of them and the person being brought back to full health. You don't need to see specific details of how this happens; just see illness dissolve and be replaced by positive energy or light and the person happy and looking well.

Then chant three times, getting louder each time if you can.

"Magick mend, while this candle burns,
Sickness will end, and health now return.
Wrap thee in cotton, bind well with love.
Protection from pain, surrounds like a glove.
May the brightest of blessings surround you in light.
For you are cared for, and this healing has might."

After the third time chanting, add the statement:
"With harm to none, so mote it be. Blessed be."

Now, let the candle burn all the way out. You can visualise them healed and happy as the candle burns down, but you don't need to do this the whole time the candle burns. You can also do this spell regularly if you feel the need.

Clarity of Mind Spell

This spell will help you in have a clear and focused mind. It is perfect to do if you have trouble quieting your mind or you are feeling scattered or anxious.

Best Timing:

A Full Moon or New Moon is good, especially when the Moon is in Libra, Gemini or Aquarius.

Required Items:

- A sage stick or another loose cleansing herb like sage, frankincense, rosemary or basil.
- If you use loose herbs, you will also need a charcoal disk
- A heat-proof container to burn the herbs in or catch the smudge stick ashes in
- A yellow candle (a white candle is a good substitute)
- A fluorite or amethyst crystal (tumbled crystals work well, but any form will work)

What to Do:

Gather your items together. Charge your candle by holding it between both hands for several minutes with the intent of having a clear, relaxed and focused mind. Once your candle is charged, do the same with your crystal. Then set your candle up in a holder on your altar or sacred space. Place your crystal at the base of the candle.

Centre yourself with some nice, deep breaths. Light the candle and say:

"I call upon the power of Air,
to clear my mind of clutter and confusion,
to focus my thinking and clear all that keeps me from making good choices.

Blow now winds of clarity,
clear away all that no longer serves, and aid me in thinking rationally and clearly.

With harm to none, so mote it be."

Next, light your chosen cleansing herb(s) and move yourself through the smoke, taking deep, even breaths until you feel cleansed, more centred, and peaceful. Once you feel you're in a better place, you might like to clear the room or the whole house with your chosen herbs.

You can repeat the invocation or take some time to sit in meditation, journal, or do some quiet contemplation while your candle burns down. If you struggle with a busy mind when you are trying to sleep, aim to go to bed soon after your spell is complete. You can carry the crystal from your spell, which is now charged up to help you with clarity of mind, for the following days or weeks.

Diet Spell

This spell will assist you in following a healthy eating and/or fitness plan to lose weight.

PLEASE NOTE, I don't believe that this spell will have you toned up and eating better by itself. But I do believe that, combined with a healthy diet and positive focus, this spell will undoubtedly help you to stay on track to become healthier. Remember that we should have a "spiritual plan" we are working with in combination with all our spells. So, healthy eating and exercise would need to be on the agenda, along with your spell (a good aim would be to start these things after you've completed your spell).

Best Timing:

A Full Moon, New Moon or Waning Moon is the ideal time to do this spell, especially if the Moon is in the sign of Virgo.

Required Items:

- Yellow ribbon or cord (you can use another colour if it speaks to you more for this focus)
- Yellow candle (a pink or white candle is a good substitute)

What to Do:

Gather your items. Wrap your ribbon/cord around your waist like you are taking your measurements. This gives you the length of your ribbon/cord to use for the spell. Charge up your candle between two hands with your intent—seeing yourself with your dream body, feeling how healthy and full of vitality you are, seeing this all happening so easily for you, etc. Take a good few minutes to do this, seeing and feeling yourself healthy and happy.

Next, place your candle in a candle holder on your altar or sacred space. Centre yourself before lighting your candle.

Pick up your ribbon/cord, and as you announce each knot verbally, you want to make a knot in your cord. (You could also add beads or crystals between your knots if you wish to as well. If you do this, make sure they are also charged with your intent)

You want your knots to be roughly evenly spaced along your cord.

The invocation is as follows (feel free to tweak the words to suit):

"By the knot of one, my overeating is done. [tie a knot]
By the knot of two, exercise I regularly do. [tie a knot]
By the knot of three, my food is fat-free. [tie a knot]
By the knot of four, I hydrate more. [tie a knot]
By the knot of five, feeling more alive! [tie a knot]
By the knot of six, my metabolism I now fix. [tie a knot]
By the knot of seven, treating my body like heaven. [tie a knot]
By the knot of eight, good health is my fate. [tie a knot]
By the knot of nine, success is mine! [tie a knot]
As I will it, so mote it be. Blessed be!"

Lay your cord, which should now have 9 knots, around your candle in a circle (but not so close you might set it on fire). Allow your candle to burn all the way down. Once the candle is finished, I like to leave everything in place until the following morning, so the cord can charge up completely.

When the spell is done, it is up to you what you do with your knotted ribbon/cord. You could hang it somewhere (like in the kitchen) to remind you of your focus when you are planning and making meals. You could hang it where you exercise or carry it on your person (perhaps around your waist while you are exercising). You could hang it in your bedroom or create a special little altar for your health, which you add your cord to, along with other things that represent what you are doing for your health—perhaps an image of yourself when you were at your ideal weight previously, or an image of someone else as you wish to be, a piece of Rose Quartz crystal, etc. (Remember, an altar like this should contain some self-love to help you get to your goal.)

Element Clearing and Healing Spell

Release all that no longer serves you using the four elements. When we are clear we are able to embrace new energies and opportunities as they arise.

Best Timing:

A Full Moon or New Moon (especially if combined with an eclipse) or any time during the Waning Moon is ideal timing for this spell.

Required Items:

- A cleansing herb or resin to burn over a charcoal disk (such as frankincense, sage or dragon's blood), OR you could use an incense stick instead
- A candle (any type or colour works for this spell)
- A bowl of salt (any kind of salt: rock salt, Himalayan salt, black salt or table salt)
- A bowl of water (collect from a natural water source if you can, but from the tap will work too)
- A healing crystal to carry afterwards is also recommended (I suggest rose quartz, kambaba jasper, ocean jasper or snowflake obsidian)

What to Do:

Collect all the items you need and lay them out on your altar or sacred space. Then get settled and centre yourself with some nice, deep breaths.

Element Air

When you are ready, light the incense stick or charcoal disk and add your chosen herb or resin to the top. Allow it to start generating smoke before you hold your hands in the smoke and say:

"With Air, I do cleanse myself."

Let the smoke twirl around your fingers. Then take it slowly around the rest of your body. Feel the cleansing energy of the herbs envelope you and begin working to clear you of anything that no longer serves you. You might feel lighter, feel tingling or something similar.

Element Fire

When you are ready, light your candle. Hold your hands above it (at a safe distance so you don't burn yourself) and say:

"With Fire, I do cleanse myself."

Feel the gentle warmth of the flame. Take several minutes to visualise the flame moving through you, slowly burning away anything within you that is unwanted or no longer needed.

Element Earth

When you are ready, take the salt and begin gently rubbing it between your fingers or hands and say:

"With Earth, I do cleanse myself."

Be aware of the salt on your skin and, once more, of the cleansing energy working and gently moving through you. Feel and visualise this energy being absorbed by you and moving throughout your being. It is shifting anything that no longer serves you or is ready to be released.

Element Water

When you are ready, dip your hands or fingers into the bowl of water, gently rubbing your hands together and feeling the water. When ready, say:

"With Water, I do cleanse myself."

Feel or visualise the water energy flowing through you from head to toe, washing you and shifting all that needs to go. Nothing is left behind except positive, light, and healthy energy.

When you feel happy you have connected with all four elements individually, dry your hands.

When you are ready, say:

"By the grace of the God and Goddess, I request that any energy, circumstance, or situation that no longer serves me now be released. I thank you for your lessons, but I request all energetic ties and permissions be dissolved and cleared now. You are released and must now go. With harm to none, blessed be."

Close your eyes and sit in silence for a few minutes more while you let all the elements, plus God and Goddess, work to clear you in combination. At this time, be open to the energy and any messages that might come through to you. You may see colours or images, hear words, and feel emotions. You may feel things shifting or feel lighter. You may even feel the need to repeat this statement more than once, or more words could surface that you feel the need to say, etc. Trust your intuition on what you need here. Allow whatever needs to occur for you. Take as much time as you need.

Lastly, when you feel ready, say:

"Dearest God and Goddess, I do now request healing and light, please. May I be filled with Source light and given guidance for the next step. I give thanks and gratitude, blessed be."

This time, visualise healing energy and light radiating down through the top of your head and filling you up completely. If you are trained in a healing modality, you may also like to give yourself some hands-on healing while this is occurring. Be open to the experience once again, allowing any words, images, or inspiration to come through during this time.

Journal writing or soaking in a bath would be perfect to follow on from this spell. Carry a nurturing crystal, like rose quartz, kambaba jasper, or ocean jasper (which is ideal for aiding the releasing process, too).

Healing Grief Spell

This spell is effective for sending healing to another person who is struggling with grief. It can also be adapted to help heal your own grief.

Best Timing:

A Full Moon or during the Waning Moon is good timing for this spell.

Required Items:

- A pink or white candle
- Rose quartz and/or a black obsidian crystal (any form you like)
- A photo of the person you wish to send the healing to

What to do:

Firstly, charge the candle between two hands with your intent to help heal this person. See them happy, smiling, uplifted, and enjoying life again. Charge your crystal and the photo of the person in the same way. Then set up your candle on your altar or sacred space, and place the photo under or beside your candle. Add your crystal so that it sits at the base of the candle.

Centre yourself and, when ready, light the candle and say:

"Dearest Angels of Healing Light,
Bring now waves of love, peace, and healing energy.
I request you send your blessings and love for this person [or use their name].
Send them your powerful medicine of upliftment.
May it be waves of positive energy experienced by them.
For I believe that [name of person] deserves a good life that includes happiness and joy.
With harm to none, so mote it be. Blessed be."

Let the candle burn all the way down. After the candle is finished, you could do one of two things:

Leave the photo on your altar, and place the fully charged crystals on top to continue sending healing energy to this person. If you want to keep reinforcing the healing energy flowing to them, you could charge another candle and light it once a week.

If the person is open to it, you could gift them the crystal(s) to carry or keep beside their bed, bringing that healing energy more directly to them.

If you are doing this spell for yourself, charge the candle and crystal with the intent to help heal your own grief. Change the invocation to be for yourself (e.g. "I believe that I deserve health, happiness and joy"), and carry the crystal or keep it beside your bed after the spell is complete.

Heart Healing Spell (Growing Self-Love)

Best Timing:

A Full Moon or Waxing Moon is ideal, especially a Pisces Full Moon.

Required Items:

- A rose quartz or rhodonite crystal
- A black obsidian or snowflake obsidian crystal
- A pink candle
- Pen and paper
- A length of pink or black ribbon (I find paper ribbon is best for this)
- A cauldron or fireproof container
- Palo santo, sage, rosemary or frankincense incense or herbs burning in the background (optional)

What to Do:

Charge up your pink candle between two hands with your intent to grow self-love. (Consider how you might act differently if you had more self-love. How would it feel to love yourself more? Would you do more self-care or talk more lovingly to yourself? Would you have better boundaries with others in your life? Visualise how this looks, feel this, affirm this.) Then charge up your chosen crystal in the same way. Set up your candle on your altar or sacred space and place the crystal at its base.

When you feel ready, light your candle and say:

"Blessed Goddess, Mother unto all, healer and inspiration,
I invoke your magick this night/day.
As this candle burns down, my self-love does grow.
Show me I am worthy, help it sink in and become knowing."

Next, hold your black obsidian or snowflake obsidian crystal in your non-writing hand. Mentally ask your crystal to help with the healing process. Then, with your paper and pen, write down everything that occurs to you that needs healing. This could be connected to a particular relationship or circumstance. If there's more than one you wish to work on, focus on one at a time (you might even want to do them on different nights, depending on how emotional it is). Remember that no one else will read this, so don't be afraid to admit or write anything you need. Sometimes, the hardest part is admitting you were wrong or feeling bad about some aspect of the situation.

As you write, continue to hold the obsidian crystal and allow your feelings, words, and impressions to be written down. Feel them, and let them flow into the crystal you are holding. Alternatively, if you feel too uncomfortable to write these things down, you could just pour everything into the crystal and write down some keywords that feel significant to the healing.

Once you have written down as much as feels appropriate, however long or short it is, roll the paper up and tie it with the ribbon.

Next, place your paper over your cauldron or fireproof container and set it on fire while you say the following invocation:

"Blessed Goddess, Mother unto all, healer and inspiration,
I invoke your magick this night.
These feelings made my heart heavy and sad.
Burn them away now; I release and remove them.
Help to cleanse my heart and soul.
I allow my heart to forgive and heal.
For I love myself, and I fill my life with love and happiness.
With harm to none, so mote it be.
Blessed be."

Watch your paper burn, making sure it burns through completely. Sprinkle the ashes outside somewhere in the wind, and, as you do, acknowledge you have released this.

Lastly, continue to allow your candle to burn down if it hasn't finished by the time you complete the releasement aspect of your spell (it will depend on how much you need to write). While you wait, this is a good time to soak in a bath with beautiful-smelling essential oils or star gaze, meditate or do something else that is self-nurturing.

Once the candle has finished burning down, your crystal is charged and ready to help with your self-love journey. You can carry it with you for the coming days or weeks, as it feels appropriate to you. Make sure you cleanse your obsidian crystal once the spell is done, too (it can be beneficial to place it straight onto an amethyst cluster or selenite plate after the spell is complete).

Personal Improvement Spells

Rebalancing My Life Spell

This spell can aid you in re-evaluating and re-balancing your life.

Best Timing:

A Full Moon is perfect, especially if the Moon is in the sign of Libra. However, this spell can be done at any time. The Libra Full Moon is an excellent time to evaluate where we are at within ourselves and our lives. It is also a great time to see if we have that balance or what may need to change to create a better balance in our lives (work/life balance, study/life balance, or whatever this might be). We should evaluate the mental, emotional, spiritual and even karmic levels of our experience at a Libra Moon.

Now, you might ask, "Why karmic levels?" Well, karma has such an influence over our lives, which many people don't realise. Our magick should be positively focused so we don't accumulate negative karma. But more than that, what we do in our lives, in general, should be positively focused too. Everything we send out comes back to us on some level and at some time. We have a karmic bank account where we can accumulate interest by doing good for others.

Keeping a positive attitude and energy, we can create more good for ourselves and those around us. By balancing all levels of our lives—mentally, emotionally, physically, and spiritually—we find ourselves in better health, coping when the challenges crop up and finding solutions more easily. We can also better support those around us.

Required Items:

- A white candle
- Some incense that you love the smell of
- Some soothing music that helps you relax
- Pen and paper or your journal

What to Do:

For this spell, I encourage you to keep things simple. Essentially, we are lighting a candle and taking time for healing and reflection.

Charge your candle between two hands with your intent to rebalance your life and bring healing to any area that needs it. See, feel, and affirm this for several minutes.

Then set up your candle and incense on your altar or sacred space. Light your incense and put your music on softly in the background. Centre yourself as you take a moment to breathe in the incense and listen to your music.

When you feel ready, light your candle.

You could use the following invocation once your candle is lit:

*"I call to you, Wise Goddess of all creative forces,
and ask that you breathe your breath of life into my spirit.
Bring your blessings of vision and understanding, please.
Ease my mind and soul, and grant me healing, dear Lady.
Show me where my life may currently be out of balance,
and ways that I may improve this.
Remind me also of the gifts that my spirit possesses,
those unique offerings that only I bring to this life.
And when my spirit is low, dear Lady,
help remind me that I have the skills, abilities, and wisdom to create the changes
needed in my life.
With love and light, and with harm to none, blessed be."*

As your candle and incense are burning, do some Moon gazing, meditation, take a soak in the bath, give yourself some hands-on healing, do some journal writing, or do whatever else calls to you and feels appropriate for you to nurture yourself quietly. During this time, reflect on where the balance lies in your life and where it may be missing. Consider what might need to change and how you could bring that change in. Jot down your thoughts and any guidance or inspiration that may come through to you.

When you are finished, make sure to thank Goddess, your Guides and Angels for their support and help during your spell.

Connect to Universal Love Ritual

Universal Love is a powerful energy to connect to. When we connect to Universal Love, we can heal ourselves, send healing energy to others, raise our vibration and open our hearts to receive love from others.

Best Timing:

The New Moon, especially if the Moon is in the sign of Aquarius, Cancer, or Pisces, is best. But this spell can be done at any time.

Required Items:

- A pink or white candle
- An incense stick (rose, frangipani, or lavender are ideal as they connect to the energy of love, but something you have on hand and enjoy the scent of will also work nicely)
- Some fresh flowers

What to Do:

I invite you to designate some time every day on the New Moon and the following six days to connect to Universal loving energy. This might be a few minutes in the morning or at night. Alternatively, you can do this at any time, for one day, several days, or as a regular daily practice going forward.

Charge up your candle between two hands with your intention to feel and be connected to Universal Love. Feel, see and affirm this intent. You might also like to carve symbols into the sides of the candle that represent this to you—such as love hearts, your initials, or whatever feels appropriate.

Set up your candle and incense stick on your altar or sacred space, ready to light. Place your flowers in a vase nearby, too. Take a moment to examine your beautiful flowers. See how they open without struggle. They freely give joy and beauty to those around them. See and feel your heart and love unfolding in delicate, beautiful layers like a flower.

When you are ready, light your candle. Feel the energy of love lit within you as you do so. See the flame flickering as a symbol of love burning within your heart. You could think of a specific person that you love to help you begin generating this loving feeling inside you. Then see and feel the love overflow from your heart and fill your whole being. At this time, you may find yourself thinking loving and nurturing thoughts about yourself. This is perfect.

Next, light your incense and take a moment to smell its scent. Thank the element of Air while staying in touch with this loving energy within you. Notice how you are now generating so much love from your heart that it begins moving upon the air itself. It is like a gentle breeze, slowly spreading outwards. Sense it overflowing beyond you to start lighting up the hearts of those you love and care for—your family, friends, workmates, and beyond.

As you continue sensing this loving flow of energy, it also flows to people you don't know. It overflows to the animals all over the Earth and to the Earth herself. It becomes a beautiful, powerful and immense love for all people and all things.

See or feel the whole world filled with Universal Love. Universal Love is unconditional, which means there are no strings attached. We are not bound by it or to it, and neither is anyone else bound to us by it. We love without judgment. We love without conditions being placed upon us. At this time, you may find yourself thinking about loving and kind acts you could do to help others. This is perfect.

Sit in this energy. Do some journal writing or speak to your Guides and Angels, allowing messages to flow through to you. Let the incense burn all the way out. Snuff your candle and use it again for the following six days. On the last day, allow it to burn all the way out.

Lastly, I recommend being creative, flexible, and intuitive with this process. Love is the most powerful force on our planet. You may be amazed how such a simple process like this can change you in wonderful, positive ways. Blessed be, and much love sent to you.

Courage and Bravery Spell

You might feel like it is time to call on some warrior strength and courage to carry you forward. This spell will help you to channel your fears and doubts into protection and bravery.

Best Timing:

The best timing for this spell is at the New Moon, Full Moon or during a Waxing Moon. It is incredibly potent when the Moon is in a fire sign like Leo, Aries, or Sagittarius. It could also be done at the 8/8 Lionsgate portal.

Required Items:

- A flower or flowers, fresh is ideal, all the better if they are fiery colours
- A vase of water for the flowers
- A bowl of rock salt
- Some dried thyme herb
- A red or orange candle
- An image of a fiery Goddess you are going to call on (like Goddess Sekhmet or Brigid)
- A large envelope

What to Do:

In the lead-up to doing this spell, consider anything that may be worrying you or making you feel defeated, anxious, and low. Allow yourself some space to feel and express any of these emotions. It is perfectly okay this triggers some tears. It is important to allow how you feel to rise to the surface without pushing it down or thinking it away. Instead, thank your emotions, as they do serve a purpose for us.

Then combine some of the rock salt with any of the dried herbs in a bowl. Place your flower(s) in the vase of water on your altar or sacred space. Sprinkle a circle of your salt and herb blend around the vase of flowers.

Between two hands, charge up your candle with the intent that you are protected, strong, and courageous. See yourself being brave, especially in any current situations that upset you. Feel what it feels like to be strong and protected in all circumstances and affirm this. See/feel yourself able to handle whatever happens positively.

Then set up your candle near your vase, keeping it outside the salt circle.

Decide which fiery Goddess you feel guided to call on, like Goddess Sekhmet or Goddess Brigid, and place an image of them on your altar near your candle and vase. This might be an image from an oracle deck or something from the internet.

Stand before your altar and take a deep breath. As you exhale, focus on letting go of any fear, anger, or frustration you may still be holding onto. Do this for a few minutes if you need to. When you feel centred and ready, light your candle and say:

"Sekhmet's (or Brigid's) fiery energy now encircles me.
I am a warrior, and so I set my fears free.
Flower, salt and thyme by three,
Send to me protection, courage, and bravery!
With your blessings, and with harm to none, so mote it be."

Keep the flower in your salt circle for the next few days until your flowers begin to look sad. This is your signal to gather the flowers and salt circle in a large envelope (so you can close it up and seal it with these items inside).

Then, in your mind, acknowledge that these things have filled and blessed you with the courage and bravery you requested. And, in exchange, they have soaked up all of your fears and worries.

With confidence in this knowledge, walk your sealed envelope to a garbage bin outside your home. Throw it in the bin, turn on your heel, and walk confidently back to the house without looking back.

Expansion and Growth Spell

Decide what you would like to expand in your life (perhaps a job you want to get promoted in, a house you want to renovate, your intuitive abilities you want to improve, a business you want to grow, etc.). Alternatively, you could focus on expanding your life in the best possible direction for your highest good.

We will work with Archangel Zadkiel, who is connected to Jupiter, a planet of expansion that is connected to the sign of Sagittarius. Zadkiel is an Archangel of goodness, grace, generosity, and mercy. He helps to bestow benevolence, good fortune, and justice on those who request it. Zadkiel is also connected to the Violet Flame.

Best Timing:

A Full Moon (especially in the sign of Sagittarius), or during a Waxing Moon, is the ideal timing for this spell

Required Items:

- A card, picture, sigil, or statue of Archangel Zadkiel (optional)
- Frankincense incense or resin to burn on a charcoal disk
- A red or orange candle
- A crystal of expansion (e.g. amethyst, orange calcite, snowflake obsidian, lava rock, desert rose, caribbean calcite, red jasper, or noble shungite)

What to Do:

When you are ready to begin, start burning your frankincense.

Carve on your candle a spiral image and a keyword connected to what you wish to expand in your life. For example, "psychic" for intuitive expansion, "home" or "house" for something like renovation, etc. Make sure to start your spiral from the centre and work outwards, thinking about expansion and growth.

Then hold your candle between both hands and charge it up with your intent, seeing, feeling, and affirming this expansion as though it has already happened. Do this also with your chosen crystal.

Set your candle in its holder on your altar or sacred space and place the crystal at its base. Place your image of Archangel Zadkiel near to your candle.

Centre yourself, light the candle and say:

"Dearest Archangel Zadkiel,
Bring to me your blessings of abundance, positivity and expansion now,
Help guide me to the best possible opportunities for my life,
That I may grow in love and strength,

And that I may succeed, most especially in [insert your focus here].
With your healing and guidance, I know I will blossom and grow.
With harm to none, so mote it be. Blessed be."

Leave your candle to burn out. While it burns, you might like to journal, meditate, moon gaze, soak in a bath, do some divination, etc.

Once your candle has finished burning down, gaze at any leftover candle wax for any messages. Allow your higher self to guide you as to what any symbols you see might mean. Make sure to move your candle wax around and view it at different angles to get the most symbols, images and insight.

Carry your crystal on you and/or sleep with it over the weeks following your spell to help keep the energy of expansion and Archangel Zadkiel's connection strong with you. You could also keep Archangel Zadkiel's image on your altar to aid this continued connection.

Inner Strength and Motivation Charm Bag

This charm bag is specifically designed for you to carry, helping boost your inner strength and keep you motivated during challenging times.

Best Timing:

A Full Moon is ideal, especially if the Moon is in the sign of Leo, Sagittarius or Aries. The Waxing Moon would also be good for boosting the energy of your charm bag.

Required Items:

- A circle of red material (I use a bread-and-butter plate as my template to make the circle)
- A length of red or black ribbon
- A pinch of sage and/or lemon peel (to remove negativity and clear your mind)
- A small garnet or carnelian tumbled crystal or crystal chips (for emotional strength and courage, plus energy and motivation)
- A pinch or two of soil from the garden (to keep you grounded, stable and strong)
- A piece of paper and a pen
- Add a blue crystal (optional), like sodalite or blue lace agate, if you also need help speaking up in the situation
- An image of a Fire Dragon (optional) if you choose to call on them for the spell
- Plus, choose 3 Herbs:
  - Thyme (for inner strength)
  - Parsley (for inner strength)
  - Fennel (for inner strength)
  - Lavender (for inner strength and healing)
  - Lemon balm (for emotional strength and physical energy/motivation)
  - Ginger (for emotional strength and energy/motivation)
  - Agrimony (to overcome fear and blockages holding you back)

What to Do:

Centre yourself before laying out your circle of material on a flat surface (like your altar). Charge all your herbs and crystals with your intent of inner strength, courage, and motivation. See and affirm your situation changing to positive and happy (you don't have to see how it changes, just that it does). Then place all the herbs you selected in the middle of the material.

Then say:

"Herbs of the Earth, Herbs of power, lend me your bravery and strength. That I may be emotionally strong and secure in all circumstances I might normally waiver. Assist my mind in being clear and my heart in knowing the best way forward. Blessed be."

Next, when ready, sprinkle the soil on top of the herbs and say:

"Soil, obtained from the gracious Earth, ground me with your presence. May I be as strong and secure as the tallest tree that is nurtured by your bountiful energy. Blessed be."

When ready, add your crystals on top of the herbs and soil and say:

"Divine crystal friends, assist me in my motivation within my life. That I might do what is needed with a compassionate heart and while being protected. With harm to none, so mote it be. Blessed be."

Using your paper and pen, draw a symbol you associate with strength. You could also write your name, initials, or "inner strength" on the paper. Then fold the paper and add it to the herb and crystal pile.

Next, gather the sides of your material, creating a bag shape. Wrap your ribbon around the top three times and tie it with three knots to secure it with the contents of your bag enclosed. Charge up your completed bag between two hands with your intent again, as you did in the beginning with the herbs.

As you hold your bag in both hands, charging it up, you could call on the fire Dragons to bless your charm bag. This would be the ideal time to do this, but it is optional. You could speak straight from your heart, or you could say something like:

"Dearest Dragons of the kingdom of Fire. I invite you to be by my side now and bless this creation with your mighty strength and power. Flaming Dragon friends, fill my charm bag with this energy I now request [pause and think about your focus] and lead me, empowered, into positivity going forward. With harm to none, so mote it be. Blessed be."

Leave your charm bag to charge on your altar overnight in the Moon energy before you begin carrying it. You can tuck it in your pocket or something like a handbag that you keep with you. Alternatively, if you can't have it on you, keep it beside the bed to soak up energy while you sleep.

Motivation Spell

This spell is for those starting to lose momentum with their motivation or want a boost to keep moving forward.

Best Timing:

A Waxing Moon, Full Moon, or New Moon is best for this spell.

Required Items:

- A red candle
- Dragon's blood resin and a charcoal disk
- A cauldron or heatproof container

- A red jasper or red garnet crystal (tumbled is fine for this)
- A feather (any type, you could collect it on a walk)
- Charm bag alternative to the crystal: circle of red or orange material, dragon's blood resin, peppermint and cinnamon herbs, pen, paper, and ribbon

What to Do:

Between two hands, charge up your candle with the intent to stay motivated. See yourself charging through the things you need to get done and achieving your goals, plus feel what that will feel like when it happens. And affirm this also. When that is complete, do the same with your crystal and then your dragon's blood resin.

Once everything has been charged with your intent, set your candle up on your altar or sacred space ready to burn. Set your crystal by the base of your candle. Lay your feather in front of the candle, making sure you can see it, but not so close it might burn. Then set your dragon's blood resin to burn on your charcoal disk inside your cauldron.

Next, close your eyes and take a few moments to centre yourself while breathing the scent from your dragon's blood and wafting the smoke around you. Allow this to help relax you and connect you to your magickal self. When you feel ready, light your candle and say:

"Dearest great Divine energy,
Universal loving force,
Come be by my side.
Grant me wisdom, be my guide.
Fill me with motivation and energy.
Bless my actions, words and deeds.
With harm to none, so mote it be. Blessed be."

You could make a charm bag as an alternative to charging up the red jasper crystal by your candle. For this, you need the items recommended above. The pen and paper is suggested should you choose to write the invocation down and add it to your charm bag. Lay your material on a flat surface, such as your altar. Place all ingredients in the centre of your material, gather up the edges and tie the ribbon around the top to seal the ingredients inside. Finish with three knots to keep it closed. Then place your charm bag at the base of your candle instead of the crystal.

Allow your candle to burn all the way down, with your crystal or charm bag charging overnight beside your candle.

While your candle is burning down, it is a good time to Moon gaze and whisper your dreams and goals to the universe. You could also do some divination if you need further guidance on the next step towards your dreams.

When the candle is finished, look at any leftover candle wax for any messages it might have for you. Allow your higher self to guide you as to what any symbols you see might mean. Make sure to move your candle wax around and view it at different angles to get the most symbols, images and insight. Then you can throw away any leftover wax.

Carry your crystal or your charm bag (if you made it) with you once your spell is complete.

Problem-Solving Spell

This spell will help you focus your energy on finding a solution for whatever is causing you stress and anxiety at this time.

Best Timing:

A Full Moon or New Moon is the most ideal timing for this spell.

Required Items:

- A wooden skewer, or something similar, to carve on a candle
- A brown or white candle
- A clearing essential oil like sage, lavender or sandalwood
- A bay leaf (dried or fresh)
- A black marker pen

What to Do:

Think of a problem you would like a solution to. If you have several problems going on, pick the one that is the most challenging. Then come up with a keyword or symbol that represents that problem. For example, if finances are causing you the greatest anxiety, you could use a dollar sign. If work is the problem, maybe draw a symbol you feel represents it or use the word "work", etc.

Having decided on your keyword or symbol, use the wooden skewer to carve it into the side of your candle.

Next, take your essential oil and begin anointing your candle in a circular motion, starting from the bottom of the candle and moving towards the top. As you rub the oil into your candle, see, feel, and affirm a wonderful resolution is on the way. Don't worry about the details; know and feel the perfect solution is coming. See the whole situation shifting into a positive state with all stress gone. Spend a good few minutes doing this, while holding your candle and anointing it.

Set up your candle on your altar or sacred space, ready to light.

Then, using the black marker, write your chosen keyword or symbol on one side of your bay leaf. Flip your bay leaf over and write your name or initials on the other side. Then place the bay leaf at the base of your candle.

When you are ready, centre yourself before lighting the candle and say:

"My problems today have become a great quest,
but the flame of this candle now sets my troubles to rest.
My soul's energy soothes my rapid heart rate,
And guides me to answers on a very soon date.
With clarity of thought and freedom of will,
I look for the way forward, knowing my heart will fill.
Let this magick of spirit be created and done,
As I will it, and with harm to none.
Blessed Be"

Leave your candle to burn out all the way. If there is any wax left, you can do some scrying to see if it inspires you with a direction. Make sure to move your candle wax around and view it from different angles to get the most symbols, images and insight. Then any leftover wax can be disposed of in the bin.

Once the candle is completely burned down, put the bay leaf under your pillow or onto your bedside table. Sleep with it for three nights. The morning after the third night, take your bay leaf outside, crumble it up, and allow it to scatter in the wind. Know that Universe and your soul are already working with you to bring solutions to this problem.

Try not to think too much about your spell or be desperate for a solution. Do your best to allow what needs to come to you. You may find inspiration for what action to follow will soon follow, or literal opportunities and solutions may suddenly appear.

Self-Love Spell

A spell to help fill yourself with love and nurturing and improve your self-love and how you see yourself.

Best Timing:

A New Moon in the sign of Pisces or Scorpio is ideal, or whenever you need a boost of self-love.

Required Items:

- One or more self-love crystals (see spell below for suggestions)
- A clean, empty jar that seals
- A pink candle
- Chamomile or lavender tea
- An image of Goddess Quan Yin (optional)

What to Do:

It is always a good time to do some work on our self-love!

Firstly, create yourself a self-love altar. This can be anywhere you like in your home—your bedside table, your working altar, a spare shelf, etc. You might make your self-love altar a permanent altar in your home or a temporary altar while self-love is your focus. Put things that represent self-love to you on your altar. Rose quartz, pink calcite, rhodonite, green jade and carnelian are good crystal choices. Select at least one for your altar and one for your spell. Hearts, particularly as a crystal shape, are excellent for this. Include pictures you like of yourself (it is critical you don't loathe yourself every time you look at them), sigils, symbols, or oracle cards representing love, self-nurturing, or whatever feels most relevant to you.

Next, take a clean, clear jar, write "I am worthy of love" on it, and draw any hearts or other symbols appropriate symbols. Fill your jar with water. Seal it and place it outside on the Earth under the Moon to charge for a minimum of one hour (this way, it will absorb both Earth and Moon energy).

Then boil the water and make a chamomile or lavender-flavoured tea, or if you prefer, another flavour that makes you feel nurtured. Charge your teacup with tea inside it, holding it in both hands, with your intent of self-love. What do you look like when you are filled with self-love? How do you act? How do you speak? Do you have better boundaries in your life? Do you glow with happiness? See, feel, and affirm your intent.

Following this, charge your candle between both hands with this same intent. Then set up your candle on your altar, ready to light, with your self-love crystals around it. Light your candle. At this time, you might like to invoke Goddess Quan Yin to aid you in your self-love quest. You could have an image of her on your altar as well and say something like:

"Dearest Quan Yin,
I thank you for bringing a deeper awareness of self-love and compassion into my life.
May this be a lingering and lasting energy."

Then sit with your candle, watching it burn down and sipping your tea. Take this time to think about all the things you love about yourself. Ponder all the things you've accomplished so far and all you are working towards. If a negative thought comes into your mind, try to turn it into a positive. For example, perhaps you start thinking about a time you felt you'd said the wrong thing. Shift this thought to something like, "It is okay, because I honoured myself by speaking up and expressing what my truth was in that moment, even if I didn't quite express myself in exactly the right way. But I value my truth and my ability to speak up. And I will continue to work towards being able to do this more compassionately and eloquently."

You can meditate, journal, and even soak in a bath while you sip your tea and your candle burns down. You might also like to see the healing expanding outwards from you into your neighbourhood and the wider world, bringing peace and calm.

After your spell is complete, carry one of your crystals with you, now extra charged, and sleep with it under your pillow so the healing can continue.

Creativity Faery Charm Spell

Connect to your creative self, and easily express this through the creation of this Faery charm.

Best Timing:

This spell can be done during a Full Moon, especially when in the sign of Pisces.

Required Items:

Set up an altar in honour of the Faeries, which includes two candles upon it, a pretty plate with an offering for the Faeries (such as crystal chips, honey, fairy sugar, etc.), Faery incense or other incense you like, a small bowl of water, and a small bowl of salt. Have your candles spaced enough of a distance apart so you can lay your Faery charm between them to charge up.

To create the charm, you will need feathers, ribbon, crystal chips and any decorations you want to add. A hot glue gun is the best way to stick your charm together.

What to Do:

Firstly, it is time to get creative! Make the base of your charm, attaching several feathers together at the point with some ribbon wrapped around their shafts (you will need a little glue to secure them all together). Add some crystal chips, decorative charms, or other decorations that resonate with you. Make it so it sits comfortably in your hand and looks appealing to your eye.

Then when you feel ready, light your candles and incense on your altar. Swirl the incense smoke about yourself, close your eyes, take some deep breaths, and say:

"Sacred Smoke, I honour thee. Your blessing evoked, one, two, three."

Pick up your feather charm. Then focus on your desire to be creative, and express that creativity easily in your life. See, Feel and Affirm this intent.

When you feel ready, say:

"Wise and joyful Faery friends,
Here do I bring you an offering,
I request that you add your blessings to my charm,
That this might bring creative wisdom to me."

Add your Faery offering onto your Faery altar and say:

"Assist me in unlocking my full potential,
Creativity is now essential,
For me to achieve all my heartfelt goals,
In all areas of life as they unfold."

Fan some incense smoke over your charm and say: "Blessed are my efforts by Air."

Wave your charm over the candle flame and say: "Blessed are my efforts by Fire."

Sprinkle some water over your charm and say: "Blessed are my efforts by Water."

Sprinkle some salt over your charm and say: "Blessed are my efforts by Earth."

Finally, finish by saying: "With harm to none, so mote it be. Blessed be."

Place your charm on the altar between the two candles to charge up overnight with the Full Moon energy.

Take some time, while the candles are burning down, to be open to the guidance and inspiration already coming through to you. Do some journal writing, automatic writing, painting, divination, or meditation to aid this connection and the recording of what you're receiving.

From the following morning onwards, you can carry, hang, or place this charm somewhere prominent to continue connecting with its energy over the coming days or weeks.

Protection And Clearing Spells

Anubis Protection Oil Spell

The great thing about creating a protection oil is its versatility; you can anoint yourself, your home, your car, or any item/building/person with it. Whatever is anointed will be kept safe from negative energy and psychic attacks.

Best Timing:

A Full Moon or Waxing Moon is ideal, but any time you need protection will work.

Required Items:

- A small bottle (a dark-coloured oil bottle is ideal, but not essential, as long as your bottle seals air-tight)
- Sweet almond oil
- Patchouli oil
- Lavender oil
- Myrrh oil (or frankincense oil as an alternative)
- A couple of crystal chips like amethyst, black obsidian or black tourmaline (optional)
- An image or statue of the God Anubis (optional)

What to Do:

To make your protection oil, place 2-3 tablespoons of sweet almond oil into your jar, followed by 4 drops of patchouli oil, 3 drops of lavender oil, and 3 drops of myrrh or frankincense oil. I like to add some crystal chips to the bottom of my jar for added protection. See my suggestions above for this. 3 chips is a perfect amount and will give an added protective layer. If you do add crystal chips, make sure to charge them up between two hands with your intent for strong protection. See yourself completely protected from all types of harm. See any negativity that may be around you being completely dissolved away. Feel what being totally protected feels like. Affirm that you are totally protected across all areas of your life. Do this for several minutes before you add them.

Then seal your jar shut and hold it in both hands to charge it up with your intent for protection—just as you did with your crystals.

Anubis is an Ancient Egyptian God who I find excellent to call on for all kinds of protection. He often appears as a jackal-headed man. We can call on him at any time we feel the need for protection or ask for his blessings on items we make to increase our protection.

Now, invoke Anubis to add his energy and blessings to your oil, saying something like:

"Dearest Anubis,
I call to you now and ask, please, for your blessings of protection,
To be placed around myself, my home, and my Loved ones.
I call for your powerful and solid protection,
And ask that you bathe me in your light, always.
Bless my oil and all surfaces that it touches,
With harm to none, so mote it be,
Blessed Be."

See and feel Anubis with you, bringing his protective energy all around you and your home. It is important to understand that the more we work with the same Divinities, the stronger our connection with them. This also means they can be more effective for us. So, don't just call on Anubis once (or whichever Deity you like to work with for protection). Thank him and call on him often to build up your protection (you can adjust this invocation for any other Deity or even Archangel Michael if you prefer).

Once you have created your protection oil, you can anoint anything you like. That might be yourself (I like to anoint my wrists), the front door of your home, the front gate, your car, a pendant, or anything else you want to protect. You do this by simply rubbing some of the oil on while holding your intent of protection. I like to draw a pentagram when I use a protection oil like this.

If you don't have the oils, simply use the invocation (just drop the request to bless your oil) and visualise Anubis bringing his protective energy all around your home and your loved ones, and keeping everyone safe. Of course, for best results, I would recommend making the oil as you are adding far more layers of energy and intent for your protection.

Clearing Blockages Spell

Best Timing:

During the Waning Moon or any Full Moon is ideal

Required Items:

- Either loose sage and a charcoal disk or a sage stick
- A white tealight candle
- Salt (rock salt or black salt is ideal, but any salt will work)
- A Selenite stick or wand

What to Do:

When I cleanse my home, I close all the doors and windows to help the smoke go everywhere. I start and finish at the front door, which I see as "rounding up energies" to move them out of my house. Light your sage stick and walk throughout your home, focusing on cleansing all negative energy plus anything that blocks your way forward. Make sure you get down to waft some of the smoke under the beds, into wardrobes and large cupboards, etc. There should be no place that doesn't receive some of sage's cleansing energy. Spend more time anywhere that feels a bit dark or heavy. It is nice to call in Angels or Deity to assist with this cleansing.

While you do this, you can announce:

"I release all that no longer serves me. I request that all negativity be dissolved and returned to light. Blessed Be."

Once completed, open the front door and at least a few windows to let some light and fresh air in. I always find this is the perfect way to finish a clearing.

Then, on your altar (or whatever feels appropriate in your home), place your candle with a generous circle of salt around it. Holding the selenite in one hand, light your candle and announce:

"I request that all negativity be dissolved and returned to light...
May the best way forward be lit up for me and every footstep be guided by Divine Sources. Blessed be."

Then visualise Dragons (or Angels, or whichever energy resonates most with you) surrounding your home. Visualise them pouring bright white light down upon you. Feel this energy penetrating every part of you and radiating outwards throughout your home. Be open to any messages or guidance in whatever way they may come through to you while this happens. You might like to purposely go into mediation at this point or take some time for divination, journal writing, or a combination of these.

Once your candle has burned out completely, you can discard the leftover wax and salt. Repeating the part focused at your altar for the following two nights would be nice, but go with how you feel. Make sure to cleanse your selenite at the completion of your spell as it will have absorbed energy on your behalf to assist you in moving forward.

Clearing Fears and Blockages Spell

Best Timing:

A Full Moon or Waning Moon is ideal for this spell

Required Items:

- Three white candles (the size of a wish candle is good)
- Chamomile herb, dried
- Elderflower herb, dried
- A mug or a bowl
- A strainer
- Peppermint oil
- Image or statue of Goddess Hecate (optional)
- Paper and pen (loose paper, not a journal, so you can burn it when you're done)
- A cauldron or other heatproof container to burn the paper in

What to Do:

In your large mug or bowl, infuse the chamomile and elderflower by placing the herbs in the container and pouring boiling water over them. Allow this to steep until cooled. Then strain the infusion, remove the herbs and keep the liquid. Set the liquid aside as you will be using it in your bath.

Next, anoint your candles with the peppermint oil while focusing your intent on releasing fear and clearing the negative energies and blockages around you. You should completely cover your candles with oil, one at a time, working in a circular motion from the bottom of the candle to the top. See, feel and affirm your intent—what does it look and feel like when you don't have fears and negativity holding you back? See your life free of past troubles.

Set up your candles in their holders on your altar. If you have an image or statue of Goddess Hecate, you can put this out on your altar along with your candles.

Light the first candle and, taking the paper and pen, sit and write down all your fears and what you feel are your current blockages. Write down any feelings connected to them as well. Write down any incidents that most stick in your head and why this is the case. Write down everything that pops into your mind until you feel you have exhausted this topic (you will likely feel physically exhausted at the end of this stage).

Then, when you are ready, take a moment to clear your head and refocus on your intent.

Light the second candle and, this time, burn the paper(s) you have written on, leaving them to burn to ashes in your cauldron or heatproof container. As you do so, say:

"I call on the Goddess Hecate,
Help me be calm but strong.
As I do now acknowledge the fears and blockages I hold within me.
Help them be released now,
Shift all blockages that hold me stuck,
So I can move forward, free and empowered.
Bring forth the blessings of love and success,
And help me see the good already radiating through my life.
With harm to none, so mote it be. Blessed be."

Pour yourself a nice warm bath. Add the herbal infusion you created earlier into the bathwater and light the last candle.

Then bathe and soothe yourself. See your life filled with positivity and light without the stress and fears that have previously held you back. Know and affirm within yourself that it is time for a new beginning. When the bath is finished, hop out and pull the plug. Watch the water leave the bath and, as it does, acknowledge that any lingering negativity goes down the drain along with the water. Let all your candles burn out completely.

Leaf Spell to Clear Negative Energy

Best Timing:

A Waning Moon is great for this spell; it would be all the better in Autumn.

Required Items:

- Some large fallen leaves (real ones you've collected, not fake)
- A black marker
- A white or black candle
- A cauldron or heatproof container
- Your journal and pen

What to Do:

I find the Crone Goddesses most helpful for clearing, releasing and seeking guidance for healing. I'm referring to Goddesses like Hecate, Cerridwen, Morrigan and Kali. So, you could choose a specific Crone Goddess to work with for this if you like. In that case, it is nice to have an image of your chosen Goddess as well.

Gather a leaf or two, big enough that you can write a few words directly onto the surface. Then gather everything for your spell, and set up your candle on your altar or sacred space. Place the image of your chosen Goddess, if you are using one, near your candle.

Then light your candle and say something like:

*"Dearest Hecate [or your chosen Goddess], Crone Goddess, and Grandmother of the Moon!
Wearing the black robe of night,
the infinite mystery, within which all may be known.
Hold your lantern high, and share your healing, wisdom and light with me."*

If you aren't working with a specific Crone Goddess, simply shorten the first sentence down to "Crone Goddess and Grandmother of the Moon!"

Take a moment to feel the Goddess's energy with you, before writing some keywords connected to that which you want to dissolve and clear in your life on your autumn leaf.

Then light the leaf on fire from your candle and allow it to burn in your cauldron or heat proof container. You can do this with multiple leaves if you like, or just one. So long as you feel you have covered all you want to release in the most appropriate way.

Then, when you are ready, say:

*"I choose now to clear the cords that bind me.
To release that which no longer serves me in my life.
Bless me and guide me as this is now done.
With harm to none, so mote it be. Blessed be."*

As your candle is burning down, you can meditate, journal or take some quiet time to reflect. Be open to any guidance that the Goddess may bring for you. She will likely give you signs and messages, not only on the night of your spell, but also over the coming days or weeks to help you with your request.

Pheonix Rebirth Spell

A spell to clear old energy and embrace fresh new energy

Best Timing:

The New Moon or Full Moon is ideal for this spell.

Required Items:

- Paper and pen (loose paper, not a journal, so you can burn it when done)
- A cauldron or heatproof container
- A red, orange, or yellow candle (white is a good substitute)
- Dragon's blood resin
- A charcoal disk
- A picture or statue of a Phoenix (optional)

What to do:

This spell will help you release whatever you need to shake off and step into new, positive energy for yourself and your life. The Pheonix is a powerful elemental energy for clearing and renewal; so, it's ideal to call on for this spell.

On your altar or sacred space, set up your Phoenix picture (or statue). In front of this, light your charcoal disk inside your cauldron, and start your resin burning.

Take a few deep breaths to centre yourself, before inviting the Phoenix to join you. You can do this informally, using whatever words come into your mind and heart. Alternatively, you could say something like:

"Mighty Pheonix, wondrous energy of change and transformation.
I do invite and call to you to join me this day.
Bring your fire and passion, dear friend,
Add your blessings and energy to my spell, please.
Help me blaze a path of renewal and rebirth
With harm to none, so mote it be.
Blessed Be."

Then take a few moments to feel and connect with the Phoenix energy before taking out your paper and pen.

On one side of your paper, write down key words connected to anything you feel you still need to clear and release from your life. This could be blocks to self-love, not being able to say "no" when you need to, a job that no longer suits you, or whatever feels appropriate. If you can't think of anything, you could write, "anything needing to be released at this time".

Next, flip the paper over and write keywords connected to your rebirth. This could include words like: joy, abundance, self-care, nurturing, wisdom, harmony, flowing with ease, protected, intuition, etc. Write down anything that speaks to you. You don't need to get any more specific than core energies you want your rebirth to contain. In this way, you are allowing Universe to create something wonderful for you, without adding any unintentional boundaries; I find often, if we allow it, Universe will bring us something better than we imagined. However, we have to be prepared to let go and allow instead of trying to be in control of everything.

Lastly, light your candle. Take a good few minutes or more to watch the flame and connect to the element of fire. You may even see Phoenix show itself within the flame.

When ready, fold your paper ready to burn, and light one end, using candle flame. Drop the burning paper into your cauldron, watching it burn. When you feel ready, you can say:

"Mighty Phoenix, energy of change and transformation.
Bless my intentions that I release to you today.
Aid me in releasing what no longer serves me with ease and grace.
Guide me as a walk forward in trust onto new paths and adventures filled with love and joy.
With harm to none, so mote it be. Blessed be."

Make sure your paper burns all the way through (anything that doesn't burn you might like to relight carefully), and allow your candle to burn all the way out. While the candle is burning down, it's a good time for meditation, journalling, and maybe even some flame scrying.

Over the coming weeks, watch for signs that Phoenix is around you and working with you. Try to flow with the guidance and messages that come through and the opportunities that present themselves to you.

Protection for My Home Spell

A spell to add strong energetic protection around your home.

Best Timing:

The New Moon or Full Moon is ideal for this spell.

Required Items:

- Rock salt
- Rosemary herb
- A bowl
- Loose sage and a charcoal disk or a sage stick

What to do:

Have all your ingredients prepared and ready to use by your front door. Close all the doors and windows before lighting your sage and get it smoking. Call Archangel Michael in to aid you in clearing and protecting your home. You don't need formal words for this; just think of him and speak form the heart and he will be there. Then walk your smoking sage throughout your home. You want to spread the smoke through the whole home, opening wardrobes and large cupboards, under beds, etc. As you walk, hold the intent to clear away any negative, dark, or heavy energy. Make sure not to miss any room. Don't worry if you revisit any spaces more than once.

Once you have finished cleansing your home, snuff out your sage stick, if you've used one (you can simply allow loose sage to carry on burning on a charcoal, as it will take care of itself). Open the blinds and windows to let light and air into the space.

Then find a comfortable space to sit and go into a meditative state. Determine what colour you feel most guided to for your pyramid of protection. It can be any colour, except white, green or black; I would avoid using those colours for any sort of protection. You might even decide you'd prefer to use a shimmering rainbow-coloured pyramid.

Visualise your pyramid in whatever colour you've chosen, around your home. See the corners, walls and roof encompassed within this pyramid, the point high up above the centre of your home. The base of your pyramid should be flat on the ground underneath the floor. Visualise and feel this as clearly as you can. Know that it is protective. Set the intent that it will keep your home safe from intruders, negative influences and unhelpful energies.

When you are happy, intentionally draw a bolt of lightning down from the heavens and watch it hit the very point of your pyramid. The energy generated from the lightning charges the pyramid with even more power and protection. Know in your heart and mind that this pyramid—your pyramid—has great protective power.

When you feel the pyramid is charged and ready, turn your attention to the entrance of your home most people enter through.

Ask for (mentally or out loud) a guardian for your home to present themselves to you. A guardian is a spirit being who will guard the entrance to your home, helping to keep out unwanted energy. See who presents to you for this job. Is it a dragon? A spirit guide? An Angel? A gargoyle? Allow them to show you what they look like. Feel into their energy. Thank them for coming on your request. Ask for their name, and spend some time getting to know them.

Once you are happy that it is the right energy to be your guardian, thank them for taking on this role for you. Clearly state your needs—it is important to set specific boundaries of what you want protected and what you will and won't allow in your space. For example, "Do not allow anything in that will cause me harm. Only allow in energies that are for my highest good."

When you feel ready, thank your guardian for being present and for the job they are doing for you. Then return from your meditative state.

Blend your salt and rosemary in a bowl. As you run your fingers through the salt mixture, focus on your intent of protection. See, feel and affirm this focus. Then lay a thick line of salt across your front entrance. As you do, once again, hold the intent that this entrance/home is protected. You might also like to run a line of your salt mix around the outside edge of your house and even the property boundary. I do this, especially when I first move into a home.

Once you have finished salting the door, home, or property, announce out loud with authority:

"This home is now protected,
As I will it, so mote it be!"

You will need to tune back into your guardian and your pyramid regularly. Thank your guardian for the good job they are doing (they don't like to be forgotten). You can talk to them at any time—it doesn't have to be during meditation. Call on them if you are feeling a bit unnerved and ask for your protection to be strengthened. You could even ask for guidance on what to do if something a bit odd is happening and you aren't sure. See and feel your pyramid being energised, strong and alive with protection (I make this a daily habit in meditation).

This spell is good to revisit about every six months or when you move house. When you revisit the spell, if you haven't moved house, you don't need to call in a new guardian; simply say "hello" to the guardian you already have.

Road Opener Spell

This is my version of a traditional road opener spell. A road opener spell helps remove blockages and clear the path or road ahead of you. This way, you are able to move forward in your life on a more positive footing.

Best Timing:

The New Year is a great time to perform this spell. Any New Moon, the first day of the month, or a Full Moon would also work for this spell.

Required Items:

- A white candle
- A bowl of water
- An incense stick or cone (any scent)
- A tumbled crystal (any type)
- Lemongrass oil
- An image or statue of Goddess Isis (Auset)

What to Do:

Assemble everything for your spell at your altar or sacred space so you have it all at hand.

Charge your candle and crystal between both hands while holding your intent of removing all obstacles before you so you can move forward in your life without hindrance. You can focus on specific problems/blockages you are aware of or just that energy of being blocked and stuck. See, feel, and affirm these obstacles are being dissolved and cleared so the path ahead is completely cleared. Remember, if you focus on specific blockages, see, feel, and affirm that any other blockages you are unaware of will also be cleared. Otherwise, those obstacles will shift when you do this spell, but more may arise soon after.

When you are ready, light your incense. Take a minute or more to connect to the element of Air. You might breathe in the scent of the incense or play with the smoke floating through the air to do this.

Then rub the lemongrass oil over your candle while you focus on clearing the way forward. Add your oil by rubbing the candle from the bottom and working your way to the top. Once that is done, set your candle up in its holder. Light your candle and take a few minutes to connect to the element of Fire.

Next, dip your fingers in the bowl of water. Take several minutes to connect to the element of Water. Feel the water on your fingertips. Perhaps anoint your third eye or lips with some and pay attention to the sensation of water on your skin.

Pick up your crystal, hold it in your hands and feel its energy. Take a few moments to connect to the element of Earth. Feel the crystal's rough or smooth surface. Notice how it fits in your palm and imagine how it lived within the earth before being dug up and making its way to you.

Touch or look at your image of Goddess Isis (Auset) and take a few moments to connect to her. Feel her presence with you. Be open to any guidance or healing she may bring for you now.

When you are ready, say the following spell invocation three times, getting a bit louder each time you say it:

"By the Elements of Universal Light,
I call to you, please send me your might.
And I call upon the Goddess Auset [pronounced awe-set],
And ask my spell for her to Bless.
Please walk beside me on paths that clear,
And guide me forward in ways I hear.
With your blessing, my inner light grows,
And as it does, everything in my life flows.
By all the powers of three times three,
With harm to none, so mote it be."

Close your eyes and feel the Goddess with you. Then imagine a road stretched out before you. See and feel that the road is open and clear. See and feel yourself easily moving forward down that road, without any hindrance. See yourself happy and healthy, feeling lighter and happier as you progress. You may even see some of your hopes and dreams on the road ahead. Try not to get too specific, and don't stress if you don't see them either. Know and affirm that there are wonderful things ahead for you and the Goddess will be with you all the way, supporting and guiding you.

Allow both your candle and incense to burn out. While they burn down, or when the spell is complete, it is nice to take some time for meditation, journal writing, stargazing, or taking a bath. Remember, continue to call in Goddess Isis in the days and weeks ahead. Ask for her to continue to be with you, guiding you. Thanking her for her connection and the guidance she has given you.

Psychic Spells

Add Energy to Spiritual Goals Charm Bag

Help your spiritual goals manifest faster by giving them a boost of energy with this spell.

Best Timing:

This spell is perfect for any New Moon, Full Moon, or Waxing Moon.

Required Items:

- Paper and pen
- A circle of cheesecloth material (I use a bread-and-butter plate as a template)
- A piece of ribbon or cord
- A piece of amethyst or labradorite tumbled crystal
- A white candle

Three herbs that you feel most relate to you and your spiritual journey from the list below:

- Anise (raises vibrations, good for astral travel, dreams, clairvoyance, meditation, divination)
- Basil (protects from astral attack while you dream, connects to dragons)
- Bay (protective, brings inspiration and prophetic dreams)
- Cinnamon (raises vibrations, opens intuition, helps bring prophetic dreams)
- Eyebright (opens clairvoyance, assists in seeing fairies)
- Garlic (spiritual protection)
- Ginger (helps clear delusions, brings a true picture of what is occurring)
- Lemongrass (aids psychic abilities, clears the mind)
- Mint/peppermint (excellent for psychic matters, clears the mind)
- Mugwort (aids clairvoyance, intuition, prophetic dreams)
- Nutmeg (raises your vibration, opens intuition)Poppy seeds (for dreams, visions, and clairvoyance)
- Rosemary (for dreams, visions, and protection)
- Sandalwood (raises vibrations, intuition, clearing, and protection)

What to do:

Think about how you would like to expand on a spiritual level. Do you want a better meditation routine? Improved clairvoyance? To get to know your spirit guides better? Perhaps you want to become a better tarot reader? Of course, we need to put in some work and action for these things, too. However, we can also do a spell to help add energy and motivation. Grab your paper and pen and write down what you most want to improve. Try not to select more than three to focus on for now; when we have too many focuses, our energy can be too divided to be truly effective.

Once you have your intent, choose three herbs from the list above that align best with your focus.

Between two hands, charge up the chosen herbs with your intent. See yourself meditating, reading The Tarot confidently, or doing whatever your focus is. Feel and affirm that deep spiritual connection and flow. Do the same with your crystal and candle.

Set your candle up, ready to be lit, on your altar or sacred space.

Lay your circle of cheesecloth onto a flat surface (like your altar). Place about a teaspoon of each of your chosen herbs in the centre of your cheesecloth (while you could use more than three herbs, but you really don't need to). Place your crystal on top of your herbs. Gather up the sides of the cheesecloth to form a bag shape, and wrap your ribbon or cord around the top to keep everything in. Use three knots to seal it all shut so nothing can get out.

Next, run yourself a warm bath. Add your herb bag to the bath, and allow it a few minutes to begin infusing into the water before you hop in. Soak in the water, thinking about the things you wrote down. Take as long as you like in the bath. You could even meditate in there.

When you have finished your bath, dry off and get dressed. Then take your herb bag from the bath and return to your altar. Remove your crystal from the bag and put it so it sits at the base of your candle. When you feel ready, light the candle. See and feel those things you have written down—doing a great job reading and giving psychic messages to others, meditating every morning, etc.

This is a good time (but optional) to invoke someone like Goddess Rhiannon, the God Horus, or another divinity you feel drawn to for assistance. You could say:

"Dearest [your chosen Divinity],
Bless me with your grace and love,
Protect me and guide me as I journey forward on my spiritual path.
With harm to none, blessed be."

You could burn more of your chosen herbs on a charcoal disk while your candle burns down. You could even burn it in the future as an incense for meditation or other spiritual work to help reconnect you to your spell and its intent. You could also burn what you wrote down at the beginning. Once the candle has finished burning and your spell is complete, you can carry your crystal with you in future as you do your spiritual work.

Psychic Growth Spell

Best Timing:

A New Moon or Full Moon is ideal, especially if the Moon is in the sign of Scorpio.

Required Items:

- The Star, The High Priestess and The Hermit tarot cards
- A purple or silver candle
- Pen and paper or journal

What to Do:

While this spell uses tarot cards, you could also substitute these with oracle cards that represent the same things to you. We are using all three cards.

Place your candle in about the centre of your altar, leaving room to lay your cards just in front of this. Have your cards ready, but not on the altar yet. Then invoke the God and Goddess. You could use words like:

"Blessed God and Goddess,
You who can see all and connects with both the seen and unseen world.
Please do bring your blessings for me this day
And add your energies to my spellwork here.
With my thanks, blessed be."

Pause and feel their energy coming in around you.

Next, place The Star card face up on your altar. As you do this, say:

"I add The Star to my altar and, with this action, invoke inspiration, creativity, and guidance."

Pause and feel this energy coming in around you.

Then when you are ready, place The High Priestess card face up on your altar. As you do this, say:

"I add The High Priestess to my altar and, with this action, invoke a focused mind, strengthened intuition, and connection to something greater than myself."

Pause and feel this energy coming in around you.

Then place The Hermit card face up on your altar. As you do this, say:

"I add The Hermit to my altar and, with this action, invoke the ability to interpret all knowledge and guidance I receive."

Pause and feel this energy coming in around you.

Light your candle, hold your hands over the cards and say:

"I invoke the protection of the God and Goddess,
I am open and receptive to higher levels of consciousness.
May Divine guidance be here for me now,
So that I may receive the knowledge and energy offered.
My psychic centres now flourish.
And I open all of my senses to all impressions coming through to me now..
I place this request before the God and Goddess.
May it be done for the greater good of all, and with harm to none,
So mote it be. Blessed be."

Pause to be aware of the energy that you have just requested surrounding you. This is a good time to sit with your journal and write any inspirational messages that come through, do some divination, do automatic writing, etc. Be sure to let your candle burn all the way down. You could gaze at any leftover candle wax for any messages it might hold. Allow your higher self to guide you as to what any symbols you see might mean. Make sure to move your candle wax around and view it at different angles to get the most symbols, images and insight.

Psychic Activation Full Moon Magick

Best Timing:

A Full Moon is ideal, especially if the Moon is in the sign of Scorpio, Cancer or Pisces.

Required Items:

- Agrimony herb (you can use another cleansing herb as a substitute)
- A circle of cheesecloth material (I use a bread-and-butter plate as a template)
- A piece of ribbon or cord

What to Do:

This spell is in two parts. Doing both parts together is ideal, but you could choose to do only one part if you want or split them up to do at separate times. The choice is yours.

PART ONE

Start with a bath that helps to release the fears and blocks that prevent you from sharing what you receive intuitively with others. The herb agrimony is good for this. So, add several teaspoons of agrimony into the centre of your cheesecloth before drawing up the sides to form a bag shape. Tie the top with ribbon to seal everything in, using three knots.

Run yourself a nice warm bath. Add your herb bag to the bath. Give it a few minutes in the water to begin infusing before you hop in. Soak a while in your bath. Focus on relaxing and releasing fears and blockages into the water. Calling on a Goddess of intuition to aid you in this is recommended. Goddess Isis (Auset), Hecate, Saraswati, Selene, Rhiannon, Freya or Cerridwen would all be excellent choices. So, go with whom you feel drawn. Speak from the heart, asking for their help in letting go.

When your bath is finished, pull the plug. Watch as the water goes down the drain, taking with it all that no longer serves you and releasing it for good. Dry off and change into something comfortable.

PART TWO (this needs to be done at nighttime and involves meditation/visualisation)

Go outside. I find barefoot is best for this, but you do what is most comfortable for you! Take time to gaze at the Moon. Notice her colour and size, and feel her energy as you stand beneath her. You may want to speak to her. Don't use formal words; speak to her from your heart, but your focus is on increasing your intuition this time. Take as long as you like here.

When you feel ready, stand with your legs apart and arms out like a star. Close your eyes and feel the ground beneath your feet. Become aware of Mother Earth's energy, which is there for us, always. Allow this energy to begin filling you, coming up through your feet and filling the whole of your body. See and feel this happening. Perhaps you see golden or green energy and feel your connection to everything grow deeper. Notice what it feels like for the energy to radiate through your heart space and how your whole body is relaxing. You might even notice that aches and pains are beginning to subside.

Then, when you are overflowing with this Earth energy, open your eyes and refocus on the Moon above you. Now, focus intently on the stars, starlight, and moonlight energy that is radiating down from above. It is pouring down into your body. See and feel this happening. Perhaps you see silver or white energy this time, and you feel your connection to everything deepening. This energy fills up every part of you, too, like the Earth energy.

Take as much time as you need with this. It is such a beautiful and profound energy to experience.

Once you feel ready, you can finish by saying:

*"I am ready for higher levels of intuition in my life.
I allow the connection to move through and with me at the easiest and best speed for me.
I am excited to see where opening to this part of myself will lead.
I am intuitive, open and protected.
I listen, feel and am confident enough to share what I receive.
I am guided and blessed.
With harm to none, so mote it be. Blessed be."*

Seeking Answers/Guidance Spell

This is a good spell for those times when you feel you need to sit and ask Universe for some answers, guidance and direction for your life. If you find that you have many questions you want answered, try to narrow it down to a few that feel most important. For this spell, I would use a rhodonite or rose quartz crystal; both crystals help keep you heart-centred and guide you along the path of your true heart's desires and purpose.

Best Timing:

A Full Moon, especially when the Moon is in Gemini.

Required Items:

- A white candle
- Rose quartz and/or rhodonite crystal
- A cleansing incense (or oil) that you like the smell of to burn while you work, such as sandalwood, sage, dragon's blood or palo santo.

What to Do:

Set up your cleansing incense or oil to burn in the background while working your spell. Then, between two hands, charge up your chosen crystal with your specific questions and your request for answers to these questions. See yourself having the wonderful inspiration to know the way forward. Affirm that the answers will come easily to you. Once this is done, do the same with your candle.

Set your candle up on your altar or sacred space. Place your crystal at the base of your candle.

When you are ready, light your candle and say:

*"Good Moon,
Round Moon,
Full Moon that appears tonight,
Guide me to the answers I seek."*

Repeat this invocation three times and, on the last time, add:

"With harm to none, blessed be".

Allow your candle to burn down all the way. As it burns down, use this time to do some divination with your favourite oracle deck, runes, or another divination tool you enjoy. You might also write in your journal, do some automatic writing, spend time in meditation, or do some Moon gazing (or any combination of these).

Once your candle has finished burning down, carry your crystal on you and sleep with it under your pillow or near your bed. Know that your answers will begin coming to you now that you have requested assistance. You might find them start to come immediately during meditation or divination while the spell is underway. Or you might find they begin coming to you over the following days and weeks. Not just through meditations but also in the everyday ways Universe brings messages to us, like repeated numbers, images or words, inspiration, ideas, etc. Try not to obsess about your questions/answers. Instead, allow Universe to speak and bring you what you need to know. Also, be open to Universe redirecting you to something else that might be better for you.

Amplify and Strengthen Intuition Charm Bag

Best Timing:

A Full Moon is best, especially when the Moon is in Scorpio, Cancer, or Pisces.

Required Items:

- A circle of purple material (I use a bread-and-butter plate as a template)
- Some silver ribbon (purple ribbon is a good alternative)
- Rue herb
- Eyebright herb
- Some calamus root
- Star anise x 3
- Lapis lazuli crystal chips
- An owl charm

What to Do:

Start by putting a heaped teaspoon of each herb into a bowl. Add the star anise. Use your fingers to mix your herbs together. This adds your energy and connects you energetically to your spell. While you mix your herbs, focus on your intent of amplifying your intuition. See, feel, and affirm that your intuition is flowing, you receive intuitive messages easily, and you can understand what comes through.

When you are happy, charge your crystal chips in the same way.

Next, lay your cloth circle onto a flat surface, like your altar. Place your charged herbs in the centre of your cloth. Add your crystal chips on top of this.

You will call on the Norse Goddess Freya to bless your charm bag. And you will do this in two ways. Firstly, write the below invocation on a piece of paper and fold it small enough to include it in your charm bag.

Gather up the sides of your material so your herbs, crystals and paper are all inside, and the top comes together. Wrap the ribbon around the top of the material three times and knot it three times to keep the whole bag sealed. Attach your owl charm to the ribbon.

Once you finish putting your charm bag together, speak the following invocation:

*"Blessed Goddess Freya, mistress of Magick.
She who glides through the night wearing a falcon-feathered Cloak.
I invite you to be by my side and bless this creation.
Fill my charm bag with this energy I now request [pause and think about your intent].
Guide and protect me as my intuition opens and grows in strength.
With harm to none, blessed be."*

Leave your charm bag to charge overnight with the Full Moon before you tuck it somewhere that feels appropriate—in the chair where you meditate, on your tarot reading table, or begin carrying it with you, for instance.

Relationship Spells

Clear Communication Spell

This spell can help you be heard more clearly and to better express yourself to others.

Best Timing:

A Gemini or Libra New Moon or Full Moon is ideal. You could use this spell in the lead-up to or during a Mercury Retrograde or any other time you need clear communication.

Required Items:

- A blue crystal (tumbled or rough), such as blue lace agate, sodalite, lapis lazuli or blue calcite
- A blue candle (white is a good substitute)
- Peppermint or lavender essential oil
- A bowl of water (or take a trip to a natural water source)

What to Do:

This is an excellent spell to do in the lead-up to a Mercury Retrograde. I always hope that, by working on good communication before the retrograde, I can say what needs to be said and organise myself well before the height of it, where communication can often get muddy.

I have created a spell with two parts to it. You can use either part separately, or you can use them both together, as I am outlining here. It will depend on what you feel called to do and what energy you need right now. For the first part, you will only need the blue crystal. For the second part, you will need all the tools outlined above.

PART ONE

If you can, take your crystal with you and visit a moving, natural water source, like the ocean. If you aren't able to go out, you might like to fill a bowl with water and sit outside in the garden to do this instead.

Holding your crystal between two hands, think of any blockages or issues that occur for you in relation to your communication. Perhaps you get frustrated with getting your words out they way you intend. Or you find other people seem to take you the wrong way. Pour all negative and scattered energies into your crystal.

Wherever you do this spell, take time to slow down and connect to the water. Perhaps put your feet, hands, or fingers into the water or simply watch it move, and listen to the sounds the water creates. This is obviously easier if you are outside at a natural water source. But if you are using a bowl of water, put your fingers into it, create ripples in the water, listen as it drips back into the bowl, etc.

Once you feel yourself relax, you can start to bathe your crystal in the water. See any scattered or negative thoughts you may have had recently washed and cleansed along with your crystal. Allow what no longer serves you to be released—and, mentally or out loud, ask the water to assist you. Spend as much time as you need with this part, relaxing and releasing. You may find emotions surface during this stage, which is perfectly natural. Go with it, allow, and don't suppress any feelings that arise.

While you are doing this, you could say something like:

*"Dearest crystal friend,
Lend me your power.
Cleanse and focus my thoughts in this time and hour."*

Take time relaxing by the water before drying your crystal.

PART TWO

Once you have returned home, take several minutes to charge your candle between two hands with your intent of clear communication. See, feel, and affirm that you communicate effectively, are listened to and understood by others, and find the right words to say.

Anoint your candle with your chosen oil using a circular motion, starting at the top and working to the bottom. As you do this, focus on your intent as you did while charging your candle.

When this is done, set your candle up on your altar or sacred space, ready to burn and place your crystal at its base. Light your candle and say:

*"I now call on the four elements on this Moonlit night.
On the wings of Gemini, effective communication is in sight.
May listening be amplified so what I say is heard.
May I always speak with no muddling of my word.
With harm to none, so mote it be. Blessed be."*

Allow your candle to burn out and leave your crystal to charge up overnight. Then carry your crystal with you over the coming days or weeks, especially when you know you will need clear communication, such as in a meeting, when teaching, for an important conversation, etc.

Communication Petition Spell

Communication includes the words we use, our movements, our tone, and how another person interprets our words. Good communication is essential in all areas of our life.

Best Timing:

A Gemini or Libra New Moon or a Full Moon is ideal. You could use this spell in the lead-up to or during a Mercury Retrograde or any other time you need clear communication.

Required Items:

- A blue candle
- A piece of paper and pen (not your journal)
- A wax stamp and wax seal (preferably blue wax)

What to Do:

Charge up your candle between two hands with your intent of clear communication. See, feel, and affirm that you communicate effectively, are listened to and understood by others, and find the right words to say. Then set your candle in its holder and light it. Watch the candle for a moment before taking out your pen and paper.

Begin by writing around the very outer edge of your paper. You want your writing to go along the top of the page, and when that line is full, turn the paper so the right side edge is now the top and carry on writing. Continue to do this every time you reach the edge—turn the page and continue writing. Once the whole outer edge is full, turn, and start the next line, so you are, in effect, creating a spiral of writing that works inwards towards the centre of the paper.

Write the following (or create your own words that resonate):

"I believe in a power far greater than I am, which flows through me at every moment of every day. I am part of it, and it is part of me. I now open myself to this wisdom within. Out of this wisdom flows all the answers I will ever need. Out of this wisdom flows kindness and love. Out of this wisdom flows clear communication with all I come in contact with. My words flow with grace, ease and love. I am heard. And I hear others."

Then, in the centre of the same page, write your name (or signature) and date of birth.

Next, fold your paper so that you are folding each side inwards to form an envelope shape. Fold the two sides inwards first, then the top and bottom. You shouldn't be able to see what you have written with all sides folded inwards to meet in the centre.

Using your candle flame, heat the end of your wax stick, then drop/press hot wax onto the middle of the paper where the paper folds all meet. Hold the paper down so the surface is as flat as possible. But keep your fingers out of the way of the hot wax. Stamp in the wax while it's still wet to seal your paper closed.

Finally, hold up your completed petition and say:

*"I now call for Universe's Blessings on this Moonlit night.
With the strong energies of Libra, effective communication is in sight.
May listening be amplified so what I say is heard.
May I always speak and write with no muddling of my word.
What is written in my petition is now to come to me.
With harm to none, so mote it be."*

Charge your petition on your altar overnight. You can carry it on you or keep it on your altar. Burn your petition once you feel it is working.

Conflict Resolution Spell

Sometimes, we feel the need to put some energy into conflict resolution and to embrace peace and calm. You could do this for a specific issue in your own life, a loved one, or the world at large.

Best Timing:

A Waning Moon or Full Moon is ideal.

Required Items:

- 1/2 cup of olive oil
- 1 tablespoon of the herbs vervain, lavender and chamomile
- A small cooking pot
- A strainer
- A bottle with an airtight lid to store the peace oil you create as part of the spell
- A light blue candle (white is a good substitute)
- Paper and pen (not your journal)

What to Do:

Create yourself a Peace Oil, by gathering your olive oil and herbs together. Each ingredient is connected to an element, creating a balance between all the elements. The olive oil is fire, vervain is earth, lavender is air, and chamomile is water.

Simmer these ingredients gently in your cooking pot over a very low heat until the air is fragrant. Then, remove from the heat and allow your Peace oil to cool.

Once cooled, strain your oil into your clean bottle. Make sure to label it, too, so you don't forget what you have made it for! Charge up your oil with the bottle between your hands while visualising blue healing energy surrounding and spreading through the oil. Open your heart space and send loving energy into it. Also, intend that peace and calm will be sent anywhere the oil is used.

Next, place your candle, paper, and pen before you. Write down the names of those whose conflict you wish to end, or write a few sentences about a situation you seek to fill with peace and calm. Dab the corners of your paper with some peace oil while seeing, feeling and affirming the situation resolved. You don't have to see how it gets resolved; let Universe take care of that. However, visualise everything coming to a happy conclusion with no more tension between those involved.

Charge your candle between two hands using the same intent. Then, anoint your candle with your peace oil, moving in a circular motion from the top down to the bottom of the candle.

Next, place your piece of paper under your candle and light the candle, saying something like:

"Conflict, stress and tension cease,
Discord melted, I call for peace.
By the powers of land, sky and sea,
As I will it, then so shall it be!
With harm to none, so mote it be!
Blessed Be."

Allow your candle to burn out all the way. Moongazing is perfect to do while this is taking place. If any wax is left over once the spell is finished, throw it in the bin; do not keep it. Know that Universe is taking care of this issue for you. Be open to any guidance or opportunities that may arise to aid you going forward.

Forgiveness Spell

We've all had bad relationships, whether in romance, with someone you work with, a friend, or a family member. Sometimes, things happen in these relationships that leave us with negative feelings like guilt, anger, and resentment. We might not be able to heal the relationship with that person, but we can work on healing ourselves. Forgiving ourselves is part of that healing.

Best Timing:

A Full Moon, especially if it is in Aquarius, or a waning Moon is ideal, but this spell can be done at any time.

Required Items:

- Paper and pen (not your journal)
- Black or pink ribbon (paper ribbon is ideal for this)
- A black obsidian crystal (a tumbled or rough piece works well)
- A cauldron or heatproof container

What to Do:

Write down on a piece of paper your negative feelings regarding a particular relationship that has been challenging. If there is more than one you wish to work on, focus on one at a time (you might even want to do them on different nights, depending on how emotional it is). No one else will read this, so don't be afraid to admit all aspects. Sometimes, this is the hardest part—admitting you were wrong, or that you feel bad for your part in it, etc.

Once it is all written down—however long or short it is—roll the paper up and tie it with a black or pink ribbon (paper ribbon is great for this).

Then, hold your piece of black obsidian in your hands and fill it with the feelings, words and impressions you wrote down. In your mind or out loud, ask your crystal to help with the healing process for this. Take a good several minutes here.

Place your rolled-up paper in your cauldron and set it on fire (you can simply use a match, or you might like to use a lit candle that you have also charged with your intent for this spell).

As your paper burns, say:

"Blessed Goddess,
Mother unto all,
Wise healer and inspirational muse.
I invoke your magick this night.
These feelings had taken over, making my heart heavy and sad.
Burn them away now,
Aid me to release and remove them.
Help to cleanse my heart and soul of any darkness.
Allow my heart to forgive and heal.
For I acknowledge that I love myself and I love my life.
With thanks and harm to none, so mote it be."

Watch your paper burn and ensure it burns right through properly (relight anything that doesn't burn). The ashes can then be sprinkled somewhere that feels appropriate to you, and as you do, acknowledge you have released this. I would advise that this should not be somewhere on your home property. Instead, let the wind take it away at a park, perhaps, or garden. You can ask Air and Earth to please aid the transmutation of this energy, too, as you sprinkle your ashes (this can be in your mind; it doesn't have to be out loud).

Happy Home Spell

This happy home spell will assist you in adding positive, calm energy to your home to help create a positive, calm, and happy space.

While we may not be in control of much that goes on outside our home, we are in control of ourselves and the space inside our home. So, putting some energy into our space is good for creating a positive, calm, and happy space. In this way we can be more relaxed within ourselves, sleep better and approach the day with a more positive attitude.

Best Timing:

A Full Moon is ideal, especially a Cancer Full or New Moon, or any time you feel the need

Required Items:

- Meadowsweet loose herb
- A yellow candle (you could use a white or blue candle as a substitute)
- Marjoram essential oil
- A piece of rose quartz, blue lace agate, or blue calcite crystal

What to Do:

Start by creating a "home altar". What is a home altar? This is a small table or shelf purposely filled with items representing those positive energies you want to fill your home with. It can contain anything that makes sense to you and represents what you would like to fill your home with. A great starting point is a photo or two of your family and/or household members. My boys helped me set up ours. We have a rose quartz heart for love, a dragon statue for protection, an abundance bowl to represent money flow, a toy car representing regular travel, an oracle card for good health, and we purposely picked a photo where we were doing something fun to represent fun and happy energy.

Pick out what is important to you and find things that make sense to represent them to put on your altar. Truly, the sky is the limit. There are no hard and fast rules for your home altar. You can even get the whole family involved in adding to it and creating it.

Next, gather all the items for your spell. Hold your candle between two hands for several minutes, and while you do this, in your mind's eye, see your home filled with positive energy and everyone happy and smiling. Feel what it's like when your home is happy, positive, and full of joy. Affirm this intent, perhaps continuously repeating a positive statement to yourself.

Once you have finished doing this with your candle, pick up your crystal and do the same. Follow this with your herb, perhaps instead running your fingers through your herb while you see, feel, and affirm this intent. Pour your meadowsweet out somewhere flat so you will be able to roll your candle in it.

Then, anoint the candle with some of the marjoram oil, working in circular motions from the top of your candle to the bottom. While your candle is still damp with oil, immediately roll it in the Meadowsweet. Place your candle in its holder on your home altar or other sacred space. Put the crystal at the base of the candle.

When you are ready, centre yourself before lighting the candle. As you do, see, feel, and affirm your home is filled with joy and love.

Say:

"Dearest Goddess, caring and loving,
Dearest God, strong and protective,
Visit this home and keep it safe.
Bless it by grace and your love so divine,
May all within this home prosper and be happy,
So that wisdom and joy can prevail here, always.
With harm to none, so mote it be. Blessed be."

Leave your candle to burn out somewhere safe. This takes about two hours if you are using a wish candle. Any leftover meadowsweet could be burned on a charcoal disk while your candle burns down or sprinkled out in the garden. While the candle burns down, you could do a fun activity with the members of your household to help ignite the spirit of what you are asking for with your spell. You could play a board game, watch a movie, or cook a meal together. If you live alone, you could create a vision board, watch a funny show, or soak in the bath.

Relationship Cord-Cutting Spell

Cord-cutting is a process that helps free you from unhealthy emotional bonds that drain your mental energy. It does not remove healthy emotional bonds but allows for a positive readjustment of the relationship.

This relationship cord-cutting spell is good to do after breaking up with a romantic partner or if you have an unhealthy friend or family relationship.

Best Timing:

During the Waning Moon or at a Full Moon is excellent timing for this spell, but it can be done anytime it is needed.

Required Items:

- A black candle
- Loose sage and a charcoal disk
- A length of black cord, preferably cotton, nothing too thick
- A cauldron or heatproof container

What to Do:

Charge your candle between two hands with your intention to dissolve and clear away negative energy and energetic cords between yourself and the person(s) you want to sever cords with. If there are multiple people, see each one individually as you charge your candle, or do this spell separately for each person. Please don't send them negative energy; simply focus on your intent of clearing away the cords and energy between you so nothing is holding or binding you together.

When you are happy, set up the candle on your altar, ready to light.

When you feel ready to begin, light the charcoal disk in your cauldron and cover it with some of the loose sage so this clearing energy can work in the background while you do your spell. Top up your sage on the charcoal as needed throughout your spell.

Then take some nice deep breaths to centre yourself and light the candle.

Hold up your length of black cotton and say in a firm voice:

"This represents the negative energy cords that hold me to [name the person or use a statement like "my immediate family"] and blocks me from moving forward, from being myself, from making my own choices, and living my life my way."

Set the cord alight with the candle flame and put it into your cauldron to safely burn through. When you are ready, say:

"While I do thank you for what positive you may have added to my life, I do now dissolve, cut, and release all aspects of our relationship which drain, restrict, or hold me in any negative state."

At this point, try to ensure the cord is burnt as much as possible. Relight any parts that need it. When you are happy, add more sage to your charcoal disk and move the smoke from the sage over yourself to clear and uplift the energy around you. Feel your energy get lighter as you do this.

Then, when you feel ready, say:

"I do now claim back my power and sovereignty. With blessings from Universe [God/Goddess], I will move forward now in light and freedom. With harm to none, so mote it be. Blessed be."

Flush the ash and any remnants of the cord down the toilet. Let your candle burn out all the way. Know that this is done. If you feel called to, you could also cleanse your whole house with the sage to finish.

Wealth And Manifesting Spells

Add Energy to a Desire

This simple candle spell helps you manifest a desire. It can give you the energy and motivation to start something new, add expansion energy to something, or help manifest a physical thing, like a car or holiday.

Best Timing:

This spell is best done on a Leo, Aries or Sagittarius Full Moon, but you could adjust the invocation to use at any New or Full Moon.

Required Items:

- A red candle
- Three clear quartz points
- A picture or item that represents what you are trying to manifest

What to Do:

This spell uses an item that represents what you want to manifest. This could be a photo or a physical item. Whatever you choose, it should connect in some way to what you are requesting. For example, if your aim is motivating yourself, you could use a photo of yourself, or, if you are trying to add expansion energy to a new business, you could use a business card or logo. If you are trying to get a new job, pick something that represents the type of new job you want. For a new car, use a photo of the type of car you'd like. And so on. The sky is the limit; what is important is the reason you choose the item. It must make sense to you.

Assemble your items on your altar or sacred space. Hold the candle between two hands and see, feel and affirm for several minutes what you want to manifest (this is your focus). Then place your candle on your altar and place your item representing this desire next to the candle.

Charge your clear quartz points in the same way you did your candle before placing them evenly spaced around it. The points should face inwards towards the candle.

Then light your candle and have palms forward, facing the candle flame, while you speak directly to Universe with the following words:

*"Dear Gracious Universal Light,
On this evening of Leo, with Sun energy burning bright,
Grant me this blessing that abundance of all I ask comes my way,
May new beginnings and energy come with the dawning of the new day.
With harm to none, but guidance for the best way forward, Blessed be."*

Leave your candle to burn out. Journal writing, planning, or meditation are all perfect to do as your candle is burning. For example, if you want to manifest a holiday, start brainstorming and planning for it while your candle is burning. Or, write a list of all the attributes you wish your new car to have. You could also do some divination, asking for guidance about the next step to help you in this manifesting process.

Once your spell is complete, try not to obsess about it. Be open to ideas, inspiration, guidance, and opportunities to help make your request come to fruition.

Money Frog Spell

I always find the energy of Taurus perfect for manifesting material acquisitions and money. This is my version of a money frog spell, and I find it cute and effective! I hope you find it draws money for you too. A number of ancient cultures believe frogs are a symbol of prosperity and abundance. So, how perfect is it to include an image of a frog in your money magick?

Best Timing:

A Full Moon or New Moon is ideal, especially when the Moon is in the sign of Taurus (my favourite money moon!), Capricorn or Virgo.

Required Items:

- A plate (bread-and-butter size is perfect for this)
- A frog statue or pendant (big enough to fit on your plate)
- Ground cinnamon
- Ground nutmeg
- Ground cloves
- A jar to store the money powder you create
- Some gold coins (and some foreign coins if you have them)

What to Do:

Gather everything you need for your spell. The best place to do this spell is somewhere you can have the frog facing the front door. You may want to create a "money altar" to set your spell on, which is in the best position for your frog. It can be anywhere in the room to be able to face the front door; it doesn't need to be directly opposite the door.

Dress your money altar with green, gold or red cloth and have other items representing money and wealth on the altar. You might have oracle cards that represent this for you, along with a citrine cluster, jade elephant, golden bee, feng shui money tree, or whatever speaks to you.

Next, you want to make some money powder for yourself. You will do this by combining your cinnamon, nutmeg and cloves. Two teaspoons of each should be plenty. Mix them in a bowl first, so you can run your fingers through the herbs, charging them with your intent of money. See, feel, and affirm your intent. Though, try to avoid focusing on a dollar amount.

Make your focus on what it would look like if money were no issue. What would you buy? What would you do? How would life look different? Focusing in this way will more strongly ignite the feelings for wealth and, therefore, bring more money to you more easily. Then, when you are satisfied it is charged up and mixed well, put it in your jar and make sure to label it as "money drawing powder".

Put your plate in the centre of your money altar. Spread the coins on your plate and place your frog sitting on top of some of the coins in its centre, preferably facing the door.

Sprinkle some money drawing powder on and around your frog. As you do, visualise money flowing to you and you being able to pay your bills or buy whatever you are wanting the money for. Take a good several minutes to see, feel and affirm this; this is what will really magnetise the abundance for you.

About once a week, add a few more coins to the plate and sprinkle the frog and plate with more powder. Each time you do this, see, feel, and reaffirm your intent for a few minutes.

Finally, avoid obsessing about your money altar or your spell. And don't forget to be open to prosperity opportunities; be ready to seize them when they come. They may come through discounts, finding money on the ground, being offered an extra shift at work, etc. Remember to take time for gratitude as the money flows in for you, too.

Money Basil Spell

This is a great money spell to do. It's not too hard, either. This is an alternative to the Frog Money Spell.

Best Timing:

A Full Moon or New Moon is ideal, especially when the Moon is in the sign of Taurus (my favourite money moon!), Capricorn or Virgo.

Required Items:

- A bunch of fresh basil (or at least a few leaves)
- A green or gold candle
- Some sesame seeds

What to Do:

Charge up your candle between two hands with your intent for money and wealth. See, feel, and affirm money flowing in for you and filling your pockets, wallet, and bank account. See all your bills paid and money left over for things you'd like to buy. Feel how this makes you feel as well. Then do the same, charging up your basil.

Set up your candle on your altar or sacred space, ready to light. Place your fresh basil beside your candle, but not so close that you will set it on fire as the candle burns down.

Next, sprinkle a circle of sesame seeds around your candle and basil. As you do, reconnect to your intent. Then, once you have taken a good few minutes seeing, feeling, and affirming this and feel ready, say:

*"Dearest Divinities of Abundance and Wealth,
Please connect me to your energy and help me create a secure money flow.
Help ease my stress, and allow financial worries to go!
Grant me the ability to have all my needs covered,
Plus, still have money to enjoy my life and share my prosperity with others.
With harm to none, so mote it be! Blessed be."*

Allow your candle to burn out all the way. If there is leftover wax, it is perfect to do some wax scrying and observe the images and impressions you see. Finally, try not to obsess about your money altar or your spell. Don't forget to be open to prosperity opportunities and be ready to seize them when they come. They may present through discounts, finding money on the ground, being offered an extra shift at work, etc. Remember to make time for gratitude as the money flows in for you, too.

Wish Box Manifesting Spell

A great manifesting spell is using a "wishing box". You can use any box you like—you might have a trinket box you want to devote to this, decorate a wooden box you find for this job, or anything that speaks the most to you.

Best Timing:

A Full Moon, New Moon or Waxing Moon is ideal timing for this spell, especially when the Moon is in the sign of Taurus, Capricorn, or Virgo.

Required Items:

- A small box
- A piece of clear quartz or a piece of turritella agate (rough or tumbled works fine)
- A white candle
- Pen and paper (not your journal)

What to Do:

Once you have decided what you will use for your wish box and created it (if necessary), gather all the items for the spell.

Think about what you want and write it down in as much detail as possible. As you write, continue thinking about what you desire, envisioning it happening, and how you feel as it is happening. It is best to focus your list on just a few things at a time—a holiday, bracelet, workshop, etc.

I have found this spell, particularly this part of the process, to be exceptional for manifesting. If you need to find a new home, for instance, write many dot points about your new home—where it might be, how many bedrooms and bathrooms, gas or electric cooking, big backyard, etc. Does it have a garage, carport, or a shed out the back? Is it modern or a fixer-upper? Consider all the details, including how much rent or what the price will be under. Approach any manifestation in much the same way. Take your time and list all the details.

Next, create your invocation for the main item(s) you wish to manifest for yourself (do this separately for each item). For this, I have found something like the following is ideal (replace my example in the brackets with what you are manifesting):

*"Universe knows how to connect me with the perfect [holiday] for my needs and desires.
It reveals to me the right next steps to discovering [the holiday] that includes everything I most desire for the good of myself and all of my loved ones involved.
I am so grateful for the path that is now unfolding before me, which will lead me directly to this wonderful [holiday] so quickly and easily.
As I will it, so mote it be. Blessed be."*

Once you have your invocation how you want it, write it down on a separate piece of paper. Then, hold your crystal between two hands and, for several minutes, think about what you are asking for coming to fruition. What does it look like? What does it feel like? Affirm it is coming to you now. Then, do the same with your candle.

Next, set your candle on your altar or sacred space, ready to light. Place your wish box near the candle. Fold up your list of things you want to manifest so it will fit inside your wish box, and tuck it away inside.

Light your candle and read your prepared invocation out loud with feeling. Place the invocation inside the wish box, and then place your crystal on top of the pieces of paper. Close the box and put your power hand on top (this is usually whichever hand you write with). See the whole box charging up with energy for the Universe to supercharge your request and manifest it quickly. Leave the candle to burn out near your wish box and leave your wish box on your altar or sacred space.

Once your wishes have been fulfilled, what you do with the papers inside the box is up to you. I like to burn them and scatter the ashes in the garden.

Plant Manifesting Spell

We can powerfully manifest our hopes and dreams by drawing on the element of the Earth. I love using plants for this!

Best Timing:

A Full Moon, New Moon, or Waxing Moon is ideal timing for this spell, especially when the Moon is in the sign of Taurus, Capricorn or Virgo.

Required Items:

- A pot for your plant
- Some potting mix or soil from the garden
- Some seeds of any plant you feel drawn to grow
- A moss agate crystal
- A small container of water to water your plant with

What to Do:

Firstly, decide what dream or goal you would like to make the focus for your spell. Select just one you will focus your energy on.

Then, fill your pot with your chosen soil. Make a small hole for the seeds to be nestled into the soil.

Between two hands, charge your crystal with your intention to achieve the goal you decide on for your spell. See yourself having achieved or purchased that thing. Feel what it would be like to achieve it. Repeatedly affirm your intent using a positive statement as if you have already achieved it. Take several minutes to do this before you put down your crystal. Do the same with some of your seeds (always plant 2-3 seeds to help ensure at least one will grow).

Drop the seeds into the hole you prepared. Gently cover them with soil. Place your hands over the pot with your palms facing downwards towards the planted seeds just. Place your crystal on top of the soil, but not over the seeds (more towards the edge of your pot). When ready, say:

"Dear Earth and seeds, may you Grow and Sprout,
And as you do shall I prosper within and without.
Earth, crystal and seeds, I do now enchant,
I transform you into my Manifesting Plant.
Grow lush, grow well, bring my request to me,
As I will it so mote it be!"

See, feel, and affirm your plant is growing strong and well. Again see, feel, and affirm your goal being made manifest (achieved). Then finally, when you feel ready, pour water on the soil and say:

"With blessings from all the Elements to nurture and keep us both—Sun's Fire to warm and encourage us, Water so we may unfurl and grow, Earth to strengthen and support us, and Air to help lift us upwards. With harm to none, so mote it be. Blessed be."

Put your pot somewhere it will get plenty of sunlight and remember to take care of it. As the plant grows, your requested dream should manifest for you.

Invoking Blessings

I love to invoke deity and other high-vibrational beings to bless myself, my work, or the items I am using. It is a way to add strong intent to aspects of your day. You can do this with formal words or something spoken straight from the heart.

When I say "high-vibrational beings", I mean energies like Ascended Masters, elemental beings (like Dragons and Unicorns), and Starbeings (like Sirians and Pleiadians). Know that you can invoke blessings from more than Gods and Goddesses. It really is a personal choice who you feel guided to call on.

The more we work with and call on the same high-vibrational being, the more we build a stronger connection with that energy. And, therefore, the more we will feel them and experience them in our life. So, if you are new at magick, definitely try calling on a few different beings to see how you find the connection. Eventually, it is good to settle on a couple that you prefer, who you can call on regularly.

Don't feel like you are annoying them or inconveniencing them either. In my experience, high-vibrational beings love to speak with us, aid us and create connections with us.

I would add that just because we are not at home by our altar does not mean we cannot invoke energies throughout our day. We can certainly invoke them at any time, and without any tools or altar. I talk to the beings often across my day and enjoy the interaction and guidance on the go! But it is nice to dress our altar and invoke blessings purposely like this, too.

Next, I will give you a basic rundown of what I do to invoke blessings. And then, I will take you through some specific energies you might invoke, and for what purpose, with specific words you could use. Please note that, with each example I have provided, there are many more focuses you could use for each being or divinity. I am simply honing in on one for you to get a good sense of what you could do and say.

General Practice:

Dress your altar appropriately for the being you are calling on. This can be as elaborate or as simple as you like. It is good to research the divinity or energy you want to invoke, so you can see what colours, items, and animals are traditionally connected to them to help you decorate your altar. Of course, make sure to have a statue or image of the deity or high-vibrational being you want to request your blessing from front-and-centre on your altar.

I also like to have a candle or two on my altar. A tealight candle works fine for this. Place the candle in front of the statue/image of your divinity.

Sit before your altar and light the candle. Take several deep breaths to centre yourself. See yourself connected to both the Earth and the Universe/Source/All That Is. Then, focus on your heart space and ensure that it is open and flowing with energy.

Next, focus on your chosen divinity. Ask them, by name, to be with you and present now. You might see or feel them appear in spirit with you, stepping close.

Then, have a conversation with the deity, making sure to ask for your specific wish/intent. Perhaps request them to be with you throughout the day ahead, protecting and guiding you. It is also good to thank them for their presence in your life.

You can sit with this for several minutes. Or even do a meditation with them for longer. When ready, thank the divinity for their presence.

It is that easy. You could do it as a five-minute practice to start your day, or a longer practice when you have more time to devote to the connection.

DRAGONS

I personally work with Dragons all the time—in my magick, meditations, and in everyday life. I find them wonderful, powerful and protective companions. They can add blessings and energy to any spell or magick work.

Because they are such a big part of my life, I wanted to make sure I started with some invocations you could use that call on the energy of Dragons. A Dragon oracle deck can be a good way to have images of the various types of Dragons to use for your altar.

Water Dragons

For this invocation, we will call on the Water Dragons to help with understanding dreams and intuitive messages.

Best Timing:

This can be done before bed (especially if your focus is on understanding your dreams), before doing divination (i.e. a tarot reading), before meditation, or whenever feels appropriate.

Dressing Your Altar Suggestions:

- An image or statue of a Dragon, all the better if it is a water dragon
- A blue, green or teal cloth

Items that represent the element Water, such as:
- A bowl of water
- An image of the sea or a lake
- Shells
- The alchemical symbol for water
- Coral
- Driftwood
- River pebbles
- Flowers floating in water

Suggested Extra Items:

- Frankincense essential oil

What to Do:

Dab some frankincense oil onto your wrists and inhale it's scent as you centre yourself. Move your hands through your aura gently; this helps put the intuitive energy of the frankincense oil through your aura.

When ready, say:

"Blessed Dragon Friends,
Beings of all the Watery Realms, with your gentle showers and flowing streams. Come. Be welcome in my sacred space." [PAUSE]

"Dear Dragon friends, please open my heart and wash away all doubt and blockages that stop me from embracing my intuitive self. Help me to easily understand the messages and guidance coming through. Show me what it is that I need to know.
With gratitude, and harm to none. Blessed be"

Pause for at least a few minutes with your eyes closed, feeling the energy of your request. You may get an intuitive impression from the Dragons—a strong feeling that they are with you, feeling a hug from them, energy in your third eye or crown, etc. You can have more of a conversation with them if you like.

Then, when you are ready, thank them for their presence.

Fire Dragons

You can add additional energy to any of your spells by invoking the Fire Dragons to aid your magickal workings. Here is the perfect way to do this.

Best Timing:

This can be done prior to any spell or magickal workings.

Dressing Your Altar Suggestions:

- An image or statue of a Dragon, all the better if it is a fire dragon
- A red or orange cloth

Items that represent the element Fire, such as:
- Extra candles
- Sand
- A pyramid
- Burning herbs in a cauldron
- The alchemical symbol for fire
- An image of a dessert or fire

What to Do:

Centre yourself, light the candle(s) and say:

"Blessed Dragon Friends,
Beings of Fire, the Spark of Creation that both inspires and banishes the darkness.
Come. Be welcome in my sacred space." [PAUSE]

*"Dear Dragon friends,
Lend your energy to my magickal work being done here.
Whisper your wisdom so I might be guided to powerful, perfect and positive ways forward.
May your energy quicken the effects of the spell I do now.
With gratitude and harm to none. Blessed be."*

Pause for at least a few minutes with your eyes closed, feeling the energy of your request. You may get an intuitive impression from the Dragons—a strong feeling that they are with you, feeling a hug from them, energy in your third eye or solar plexus, etc. You can have more of a conversation with them if you'd like.

Then, when you are ready, thank them for their presence. And follow this invocation with your spell.

Earth Dragons

You can invoke the Earth Dragons to aid you in your garden. They help the plants to grow and flourish. Earth Dragons work happily with other elementals like Faeries, too. Here is the perfect way to do this.

Best Timing:

This can be done before going outside, doing gardening, or caring for a plant struggling to stay alive.

Dressing Your Altar Suggestions:

- An image or statue of a Dragon, all the better if it is an Earth Dragon
- A green or brown cloth

Items that represent the element earth, such as:
- A bowl of dirt
- A vase of flowers
- A pot plant
- Crystals
- The alchemical symbol for earth
- Rocks
- Bark
- Sticks
- Pinecones

What to Do:

You might feel called to stand or sit out in the garden or beside whatever plant(s) you want the Earth Dragons to help you with rather than being by your altar. Go with it if that is what you feel. Or you might create this altar outside in the garden.

Centre yourself and say:

*"Blessed Dragon Friends,
Beings of Earth, with your steadfast strength and gentle nurturing. Come. Be welcome in my sacred space."* [PAUSE]

*"Dear Dragon Friends, Lend your energy to my herbs, plants and green places. May they grow in strength, grow in health, may they grow and thrive. Help guide me as to when is most appropriate to water and when my plants have other needs requiring to be met.
With gratitude and harm to none. Blessed be."*

Pause for at least a few minutes with your eyes closed, feeling the energy of your request. You may get an intuitive impression from the Dragons—a strong feeling that they are with you, feeling a hug from them, energy in your heart space, etc. You can have more of a conversation with them if you'd like. Or, if you start feeling guided to things that need doing in the garden, flow with that, especially while the energy is strong.

Then, when you are ready, thank them for their presence.

Air Dragons

You can invoke the Air Dragons to help inspire you. This can be done when you need to do some writing, poetry, arts and crafts, a project, or whatever you feel some inspiration will be helpful for.

Best Timing:

This can be done before you do any form of writing, dance, speech, performance or something you want inspiration for. This could even be done at the start of the day.

Dressing Your Altar Suggestions:

- An image or statue of a Dragon, all the better if it is an Air Dragon
- A purple, yellow or white cloth

Items that represent the element Air, such as:
- Burning incense
- Feathers
- A bell
- Photos of clouds, mountain peaks or storms
- The alchemical symbol for air

Suggested Extra Items:

- Bergamot essential oil

Preferably, sit in front of something that represents what you are seeking inspiration for (e.g. your pen and paper).

What to Do:

Dab some bergamot oil onto your wrists and inhale its scent as you centre yourself. Move your hands through your aura gently; this helps put this inspirational and uplifting energy through your aura.

When ready, say:

*"Blessed Dragon Friends,
Beings of Air, with your spirit of joy as you play in the breezes. Come. Be welcome in my sacred space."* [PAUSE]

"Dear Dragon friends, Send to me your sparks of inspiration and creativity. Help ideas to form like seeds, growing and sprouting with quickened pace into wondrous works of art. Guide me to new ideas with merit. Help me to see outside the box. With gratitude and with harm to none. Blessed be."

Pause for at least a few minutes with your eyes closed, feeling the energy of your request. You may get an intuitive impression from the Dragons—perhaps a strong feeling that they are with you, feeling a hug from them, energy in your heart or solar plexus, etc. You can have more of a conversation with them if you'd like. If you start feeling guided in your art, writing, or whatever you have requested inspiration for, flow with this.

Then, when you are ready, thank them for their presence.

DIVINITIES

I love to call on divinities regularly in my life. Being an eclectic Witch, I work with a variety of Gods and Goddesses from several different pantheons. If you are new to the craft, I suggest getting a feel for a few different deities before deciding on any specific pantheon or dedicating to any one divinity. That is, if you decide to settle on working exclusively with a specific pantheon, tradition, or divinity, it is your personal choice to do so.

Oracle decks can be a good way to have images of the various divinities for your altar. There are quite a few different decks available specifically for Goddesses and Gods (especially Goddesses).

Goddess Isis (Auset)

Goddess Isis's Ancient Egyptian name is Goddess Auset. She is an Egyptian Goddess of healing, magick, wisdom, motherhood, love, fertility, intuition, and the Moon.

For this invocation, we will call on the Goddess Isis to aid us as being a healer.

Best Timing:

This can be done before bed, when you first get up in the morning, or before you are going to do any work helping others—doing hands-on-healing, giving advice, being a parent, etc.

Dressing Your Altar Suggestions:

- An image or statue of Goddess Isis
- A blue, purple or white cloth

Items that are connected to and considered to represent Goddess Isis, such as:
- A lotus
- An ankh
- A sun disk
- A sistrum rattle
- Isis wings
- A pyramid
- A throne
- The Moon
- A sparrowhawk or kite
- An Isis-faced clear quartz or lapis lazuli crystal

Suggested Extra Items:

- Blue lotus or frankincense essential oil

What to Do:

Dab some of the essential oil onto your wrists and inhale its scent as you centre yourself. Move your hands through your aura gently; this helps put this high-vibrational energy from the oil through your aura.

When ready, say:

"Dearest Goddess Isis [or "Auset", pronounced awe-set]
Open my eyes to the wonders and miracles of all life everywhere,
Open my heart to the powerful pulse of creation,
Open my ears to the needs of others with compassion,
Open my spirit to intuition, Source Light, energy and flow,
May I be a positive instrument of support and healing here upon the Earth,
May I be a humble gift to all I meet and am guided towards,
May you, dear, wise and powerful Mother Goddess, work through me always,
With gratitude, and harm to none. Blessed be."

Pause for at least a few minutes with your eyes closed, feeling the energy of your request. You may get an intuitive impression from Goddess Isis or some guidance and inspiration coming through from her. You can have more of a conversation with her if you like.

Then, when you are ready, thank Goddess Isis for her presence.

Goddess Brigid

Goddess Brigid is a Celtic Goddess of healing, music, poetry and inspiration, prophecy, fertility and childbirth, kitchen witchcraft, holy wells, the hearth, protection and smith crafts.

For this invocation, we will call on the Goddess Brigid to bless our cooking.

Best Timing:

This can be done before we go into the kitchen to cook a meal. You could set your altar to Goddess Brigid in a corner of your kitchen so you can more easily feel her connection while you are cooking.

Dressing Your Altar Suggestions:

- An image or statue of Goddess Brigid
- A red, green, or white cloth

Items that are connected to and considered to represent Goddess Brigid, such as:
- A Brigid's cross
- A red candle
- A flame
- A corn dollie
- A serpent
- Dandelions
- Snowdrops

- Oak leaves
- The lark (bird)
- Water collected from a holy well
- A fire agate or carnelian crystal.

Suggested Extra Items:

- Lavender essential oil
- You will need a candle to light in honour of Goddess Brigid

What to Do:

Dab some of the essential oil onto your wrists and inhale its scent as you centre yourself. Move your hands through your aura gently; it helps put this beautiful energy from the oil through your aura.

When ready, say:

"Dearest Brigid, Goddess of hearth and fire,
I call to you and honour you by lighting this sacred flame [PAUSE and light your candle]
Help me in activating my own inner fire,
And bless my hands as they work to create a delicious feast,
From the gifts of your great abundance, the fertility of the Earth.
Thank you for sustaining our lives with these gifts of life-sustaining food.
May this food be filled with love, joy, abundance and nourishment for all who eat it.
With gratitude and harm to none. Blessed be."

Pause for at least a few minutes with your eyes closed, feeling the energy of your request. You may get an intuitive impression from Goddess Brigid or some guidance and inspiration coming through from her. You can have more of a conversation with her if you like. If you start feeling guided in your baking, cooking, or preparing of food, flow with this.

Then, when you are ready, thank Goddess Brigid for her presence.

God Poseidon

The God Poseidon is a Greek God of the sea, the Earth, fertility, earthquakes, storms, floods, drought and horses, as well as a protector of sailors.

For this invocation, we will call on the God Poseidon to aid us in working through deep emotions, like grief and trauma.

Best Timing:

This can be done when you have time to work through some deep emotions. You could do this invocation before going to counselling, any type of energy healing, soaking in a bath, journal writing, etc.

Dressing Your Altar Suggestions:

- An image or statue of God Poseidon
- A blue, green or teal cloth

Items that are connected to and considered to represent God Poseidon, such as:
- A trident or three-pronged fork

- Water collected from the sea
- Sea shells
- A horse, a bull, or dolphin
- A merman
- A sailboat
- A seahorse
- A sprig from a pine tree
- An aquamarine crystal.

Suggested Extra Items:

- Pine essential oil

What to Do:

Dab some of the essential oil onto your wrists and inhale its scent as you centre yourself. Move your hands through your aura gently; it helps put the earthy energy from the oil through your aura.

When ready, say:

"Dearest God Poseidon, Lord of the oceans and deep-sea depths,
I am done with the great tsunamis of life and request your safe harbour for a time.
Shield me from future storms as I navigate to find inner calm and healing,
Earth-shaker and wave-bringer!
You teach us endurance and patience, persistence and how to flow with change.
Guide me as I explore my own inner depths,
With your blessing, may my soul be drenched in your healing waters,
Search my heart for any open wounds and aid in the releasement of fear, anger, grief, abandonment, shame, and anything that only keeps me from being whole.
Help me to find wisdom, understanding and strength.
With gratitude and harm to none. Blessed be."

Pause for at least a few minutes with your eyes closed, feeling the energy of your request. You may get an intuitive impression from Poseidon—a strong feeling that he is with you, a cool energy like water around you, a physical touch etc. You can have more of a conversation with him if you like.

This invocation may trigger emotions to surface, so be prepared (have tissues on hand) and allow yourself some time and space after making this request.

Then, when you are ready, thank the God Poseidon for his presence.

ANGELS

Angels and Archangels are such beautiful and loving energies to work with and call on in your life. You can simply ask "the Angels to be with you" or to aid in something specific. You can call on specific Archangels to help with different areas of your life. I know that many love to call on Archangel Michael and know him well. There is a prayer for Archangel Michael, which has been around for a long time but has very religious wording. I wanted to have my own invocation to use and share instead of his official prayer. I hope you find it just as powerful to use.

Once again, there are lots of Angel oracle decks that have images of the various Angels, which you could use on your altar instead of having to buy lots of statues.

Archangel Michael

Archangel Michael is a spiritual warrior, a powerful protector, a champion of justice and the patron saint of police officers and law enforcement.

For this invocation, we will call on the Archangel Michael for protection.

Best Timing:

This can be done when you first get up in the morning, before bed, or before you head off somewhere that doesn't make you feel safe. You could also adapt this to send Archangel Michael to someone you know who needs protection.

Dressing Your Altar Suggestions:

- An image or statue of Archangel Michael
- A blue, purple or white cloth

Items connected to and considered to represent Archangel Michael, such as:
- A sword, shield, or helmet
- Angel wings
- A set of scales
- Aster or angelica flowers
- Candles/fire
- A lion
- The crystal blue kyanite or lapis lazuli

Suggested Extra Items:

- Bay laurel or sandalwood essential oil
- An Archangel Michael pendant (optional)

What to Do:

Dab some of the essential oil onto your wrists and inhale its scent as you centre yourself. Move your hands through your aura gently; it helps put this high vibrational energy from the oil through your aura.

When ready, say:

"Dearest Archangel Michael, Champion of justice and truth,
Surround me in your protective blue Light. [PAUSE to see and feel this]
Defend me now, and stand against all negativity in the world.
Use your sword to clear away all energy from any person, place or situation holding me back in my life.
Guide my attention to the positive signs around me so that I may recognise your presence.
And fill me with faith, courageous
In the knowledge,
I am never alone and am part of Source Light myself.
With gratitude and with harm to none. Blessed be."

Pause for at least a few minutes with your eyes closed, feeling the energy of your request. You may get an intuitive impression from Archangel Michael—a strong feeling that he is with you, feeling his touch on your arm or head, a hot, buzzing energy etc. You can have more of a conversation with him if you like.

If you are using a pendant, anoint it with some of the oil after the invocation is completed and wear it across the day ahead.

Then, when you are ready, thank Archangel Michael for his presence.

A Final Word on Magick and Working Towards Our Goals

No matter what type of manifesting or spellcasting you perform, your primary goal should be success, healing, and empowerment.

It is important to remember that the Universe is an abundant place. There is plenty to go around. And we should not feel embarrassed to work towards the goals of things we want in our lives. Spirit has provided everything we need to exist on this planet, and there is no such thing as asking for too much. Neither poverty nor greed are a part of natural magick. Causing others to suffer poverty or stealing from them constitutes greed, and it is my belief that real Witches don't do that. However, feeling that you don't deserve to have what you want is not ideal either.

Spirit does not want you to feel guilty about wanting to be the best you can be or wanting the best for yourself and your family. There are so many high-vibrational beings in spirit who will help you work towards your goals and desires, so long as you are determined to "harm none" in the process of gaining them. For your magick and spellwork to be successful and work consistently, you must believe with all your heart that it is okay to want and have these things you are requesting. You must recognise that you deserve your requests, too.

It is also a good idea not to limit the possibilities in our magickal work by placing boundaries on it. We don't need to control every aspect of our requests. If we place limitations on the how, when, where, and why our spellcasting should manifest, we effectively limit the possibilities and can strangle the outcome of our manifesting. The Universe can see the whole picture from a higher perspective than we can. So, if we learn to surrender our need, and allow the Universe to help design the end result, it will do it in the most perfect way and at the most perfect time (often in a better way than what we, ourselves, could have imagined!).

So, please know that you deserve to have all that your heart desires. The most powerful force in the Universe is Love—it is a potent force to bless all your magick, everyone you come across, and yourself with! Out of love comes many other powerful forms of energy like hope, wisdom, strength, compassion, trust, generosity, cooperation, and kindness. These are precisely the kinds of energies that make life worth living. Just imagine how your life can change if you truly love and nurture yourself and embrace some of the simple spiritual practices I have shared with you here.

So, don't be afraid to open your heart and your arms to accept the abundance of the world around you. Spirit wants you to enjoy your time on our Mother Earth, to do good for others AND be happy, too!

May Universe guide and bless you today and always xx

Additional Correspondences

Sometimes, when doing spells, we may need to swap out items or substitute the colour of the candle we are using for something different than has been recommended. Perhaps, after doing several of the spells in this book, you will feel confident enough to start putting your own spells together. Here are some lists of correspondences to aid you with this.

Magickal Associations of Colour

Each colour traditionally rules over and relates to various correspondences, which can be incorporated into your magickal workings. Here are some you could use:

Red: Energy, vitality, strength, health, courage, willpower, conquering fear, and sexual potency. Red can be used to counter psychic attacks. Use magenta to help speed up the actions being taken or to aid quick changes.

Orange: Creativity, attraction, encouragement, power, change of luck, drawing good things into your life, adaptability, and career. This colour can bring about major changes.

Yellow: Charm, confidence, intellect, imagination, gentle persuasion, inspiration, concentration, counselling, creativity, mental clarity, and business ventures.

Green: Prosperity, growth, healing, luck, abundance, fertility, generosity, money, success, renewal, marriage, balance, communicating with nature, and a fresh outlook on life. Green can be good to help balance unstable situations.

Blue: Protection, peace, tranquillity, truth, inspiration, wisdom, understanding, good health, harmony in the home, and patience. You can use light blue more for inspiration to find the truth and harmony in the home. You can use Royal Blue more for loyalty and group success.

Purple: All psychic abilities and intuition, dreams, wisdom, enchantment, spirituality, success, progress, protection, spirit contact, break bad luck, drive away evil, and divination. This colour also aids in stopping and lies, balancing karma and neutralising negative magick.

Pink: Love, honour, friendship, affection, romance, spiritual awakening, and healing of the heart or spirit. Pink attracts the purest forms of love – it doesn't have to be romantic.

Black: Healing, banishing, Crone magick, mourning/loss, protection, releasing, and helps repel negative magick or thought forms. Black can absorb and remove energies and spell work. It can repel dark magick and negativity.

White: Purity, truth, protection, spirituality, sincerity, wholeness, greater attainments in life, raising vibrations, balancing the aura, contacting spirit helpers, and destroying negativity. If you are unsure of what colour to use, white is the perfect choice.

Brown: Animal magick, earth awareness, financial success, balance, ESP, intuition, and study. Brown attracts Earth Elementals and is great for aiding our communication with nature spirits.

Gold: Often used to represent the God or aid connection to him, good fortune, understanding, all financial levels including career, attracts higher influences, quick money, healing, happiness, intuition and working with those in positions of authority.

Silver: Often used to represent the Goddess or aid connection to her, dissolves negativity, all psychic abilities and intuition, victory, stability, meditation, dreams, stars and star places. Silver can neutralise situations and help to repel destructive forces.

Magickal Associations of Essential Oils

Each essential oil traditionally rules over and relates to various correspondences which can be incorporated into your magickal workings. Here are some you could use:

Basil: happiness, peace, money, protection, harmony of all kinds, dragon connections.

Bergamont: money, happiness, optimism, protection, success, strength, confidence.

Black Pepper: physical energy, protection, courage, motivation, mental alertness.

Cedar: purification, healing, warding, good fortune, repels negative energy, rejuvenates.

Chamomile: sleep, meditation, peace, harmony, calming, uplifting, purification, luck.

Clary Sage: calm, dreams, optimism, protection, healing, grounding, wisdom, intuition.

Dragon's Blood: protection, purification, removing hexes, boosting/increasing.

Eucalyptus: purification, healing, growth, concentration, balancing, life purpose.

Frankincense: protection, purification, spirituality, meditation, blessing, visions.

Gardenia: peace, attracting pure love, healing, harmony, mending marital problems.

Geranium: happiness, protection, tranquillity, spirituality, success, health, love.

Jasmine: love, peace, spirituality, sleep, psychic dreams, balance, astral projection.

Lavender: healing, love, peace, meditation, cleansing, good health, dream recall.

Lemon: vitality, healing, physical energy, purification, divination, prophecy, protection.

Marjoram: peace, sleep, perseverance, healing, protection, aids grief/loneliness, love.

Myrrh: breaks hexes, protection, aids psychic development, healing, meditation.

Orange: success, clarity, joy, prosperity, love, luck, self-awareness, creativity, positivity.

Peppermint: money, purification, healing, mental clarity, regeneration, vibrancy.

Rose: love, cleansing places, fertility, peace, beauty, creativity, dispelling anger.

Rosemary: longevity, conscious mind, memory, love, protection, blessing, courage.

Sandalwood: protection, purification, spirituality, meditation, healing, past lives.

Sage: purification, finding wisdom and truth, memory, comfort, grounding, protection.

Ylang Ylang: joy, uplifting, psychic awareness, confidence, protection, Faery magick

Magickal Associations of the Planets

Each planet traditionally rules over and relates to various correspondences which can be incorporated into your magickal workings.

SUN

Day: Sunday

Element: fire

Zodiacal sign: Leo

Colour: gold, orange, deep or bright yellow

Animal: lion and hawk

Metal: gold

Crystal: diamond, amber, sunstone, golden tiger eye

Tree/herb: juniper, laurel, marigold, saffron, birch, sunflower, rosemary

General associations: strength, health, determination, vitality, optimism and self-expression. Can also relate to the arts, banking, corporate bodies, fame, fatherhood, government office, honour, leadership, nobility, being organised, how we are viewed publicly, and teaching. Sun energy can help give anything a big push forward.

MOON

Day: Monday

Element: water

Zodiacal sign: Cancer

Colour: silver, white, pastel shades

Animal: crab and owl

Metal: silver, aluminium

Crystal: moonstone (any variety), pearl

Tree/herb: willow, hawthorn, lotus flower, chamomile, juniper, wintergreen

General associations: our emotional reactions, flowing with life, inspiration, intuition, and sensitivities. Also relates to how we feel, our rhythm, antiques, commitment, increasing our perception, introspection, karma, maturity, morality, social welfare, and caring for others.

MERCURY

Day: Wednesday

Element: air

Zodiacal sign: Gemini and Virgo

Colour: orange, yellow, violet

Animal: monkey and magpie

Metal: quicksilver, zinc

Crystal: citrine, agate

Tree/herb: hazel, fern, marjoram, wormwood, parsley, lavender

General associations: communication, the intellect, healing, study, memory, hyper-activity, shrewdness, and versatility. It also relates to curiosity, invention, land or air travel, language, learning, mathematics, the media, public speaking, publishing of all types, professional success, contracts, court hearings, exams, job interviews, vehicles, and our wit.

VENUS

Day: Friday

Element: air

Zodiacal sign: Taurus and Libra

Colour: light blue, green, pink

Animal: cat and dove

Metal: copper, bronze

Crystal: jade, rose quartz, green aventurine,

Tree/herb: peach, pear, rose, carnation, passionflower, daisy, eucalyptus

General associations: harmony, growth and development, love and marriage, sexuality and union, beauty and aesthetics, music and dance, femininity, affection, materialism, make-up and fashion, personal finances, pleasure, relationships, fertility, and creativity.

MARS

Day: Tuesday

Element: fire

Zodiacal sign: Aries and Scorpio

Colour: strong reds, autumn shades

Animal: tiger and falcon

Metal: iron, steel

Crystal: ruby, bloodstone

Tree/herb: heather, nettle, dandelion leaf, ginger, mugwort

General associations: success, courage, competition and confrontation, determination, focus, an adventurous spirit, armed forces, masculinity, engineering, politics, the emergency services, forcefulness, logic, metal work, war, and sports. Mars is connected to a powerful forward movement.

JUPITER

Day: Thursday

Element: fire

Zodiacal sign: Sagittarius and Pisces

Colour: purple, blue, indigo, green

Animal: horse and eagle

Metal: tin

Crystal: amethyst

Tree/shrub: agrimony, cedar, ash, hawthorn, chamomile, peppermint, sage

General associations: prosperity, luck, charity, might and wisdom, friendship, inner and outer wealth, good judgment, knowledge, finding meaning, understanding, legal matters and justice, philosophy, grounding and stability, travelling abroad, and any other long journeys.

SATURN

Day: Saturday

Element: earth and water

Zodiacal sign: Capricorn and Aquarius

Colour: black, darker shades

Animal: goat and vulture

Metal: lead

Crystal: jet, onyx, black obsidian

Tree/herbs: apple, comfrey, cypress, ivy, thyme, fuchsia

General associations: concentration, conversation, destiny, karma, experience, overcoming bad habits, clearing negative energy, perseverance, agriculture, antiques, career status, economy, tenacity, maturity, morality, and social welfare.

PLUTO

Day: Tuesday

Element: water

Zodiacal sign: Cancer and Scorpio

Colour: brown and black

Animal: phoenix

Metal: chrome

Crystal: jet, onyx, black obsidian

Tree/herbs: acacia, passionflower, plants with a bulb, e.g. tulips.

General associations: changes, transformation and renewal, karma, secrets, wealth, justice, the afterlife and spirituality, memories and the past, wisdom, death, and rebirth.